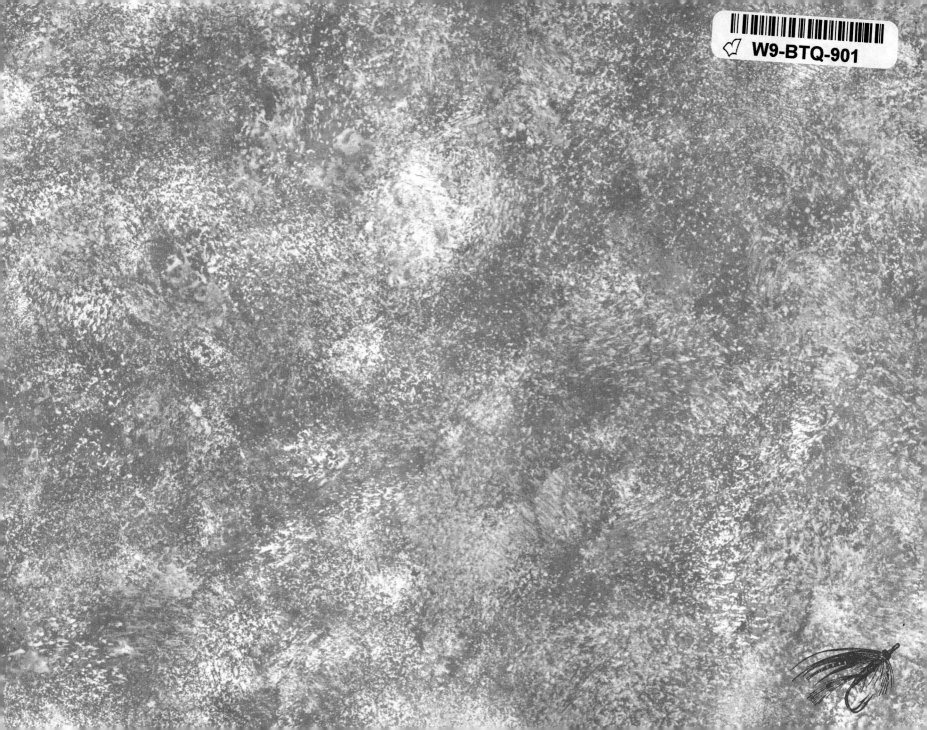

COUNTRY LIFE

The

FLYFISHER'S COMPANION

COUNTRY LIFE

The
FLYFISHER'S COMPANION

JOHN BUCKLAND

PYRAMID BOOKS

The publishers gratefully acknowledge the help and loan
of material from the following: Miss Meryl Beamont,
Librarian, The Salmon and Trout Association; Mr James
Hardy and Mr J.B. Waterton, The House of Hardy,
Alnwick; Derek Mills, historian of old postcards; C.
Farlow & Co. Ltd; Jamie Maxtone-Graham, collector
and author; The London Library.

First published 1990 by Pyramid Books,
an imprint of the Octopus Publishing Group,
Michelin House, 81 Fulham Road, London SW3 6RB

ISBN 1 85510 030 4

Produced by Mandarin Offset
Printed and bound in Hong Kong

Contents

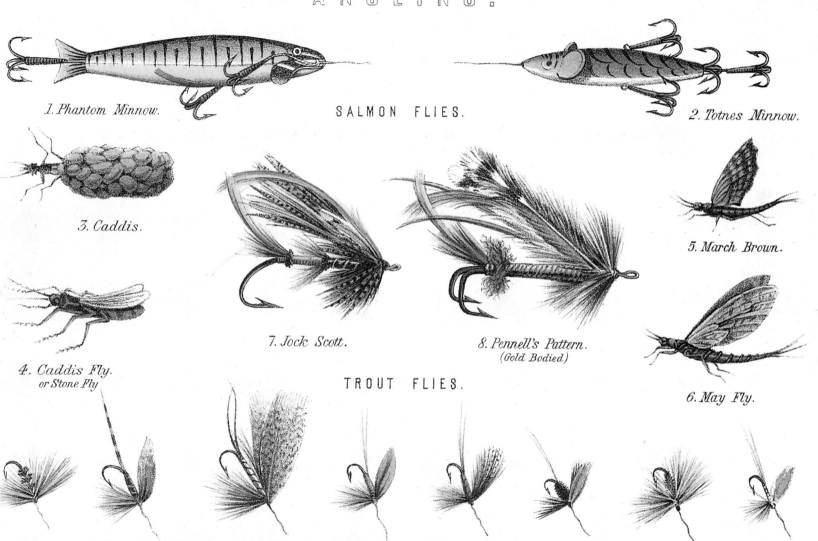

ANGLING.

SALMON FLIES.

TROUT FLIES.

1. Phantom Minnow.

2. Totnes Minnow.

3. Caddis.

5. March Brown.

4. Caddis Fly.
or Stone Fly

7. Jock Scott.

8. Pennell's Pattern.
(Gold Bodied)

6. May Fly.

9. Brown Palmer   10. Stone Fly.   11. Grey Drake.   12. Brown Moth.   13. Red Spinner.   14. Black Gnat   15. Willow Fly.   16. Whirling Dun.

INTRODUCTION

Fly-fishing has so many enjoyable aspects. The action of casting is one of rhythmic pleasure. The accurate and delicate presentation of a fly is an intriguing and sometimes baffling challenge, no less than the choice of fly itself – either to 'match the hatch' or to tempt a more predatory activity from the fish. A really first-class imitation of a forage fish that will consistently fool a trout is quite as praiseworthy an achievement as a first-class sedge or mayfly pattern.

A fly rod, particularly one in a natural material such as cane, is more than a tool. It has a life of its own, and is to be cherished as an old friend and partner. For some fishermen, a favoured rod can come to acquire an almost mystical value.

A reel too may be just a reservoir for line but it may also be regarded as a jewel of lightweight engineering, exquisitely finished and offering music to the ear.

The more enjoyment we find in our tackle, the deeper grows our pleasure in our sport – and, probably, the larger our catch.

But, of course, the ultimate fascination of fishing is the fish. Brown trout fishermen appreciate their quarry's selectivity and its wide variation in markings. Rainbow trout fishermen value their fish for its vigour and willingness to move to a fly. Those who fish for wild brook trout savour its rich palette of colours – and mourn the destruction of so many of the rivers and streams where this sensitive creature formerly flourished. The salmon fisherman delights in the sleek mysterious wanderer of the open ocean which returns against all odds to take his fly in the river of its birth. For each fisherman there is the challenge of meeting a quarry in its own environment, a quarry sharp in instinct and reflex at keeping itself alive. He must also meet equably this challenge in which so often and so frustratingly he is the loser.

Whatever our tastes in sense or scenery – and some people are happy fishing in a concrete reservoir – fishing offers us also a range of physical and mental challenges and, at the end of the day, a quite extraordinary sense of satisfaction.

Part of the fascination of fishing lies in the fly – or lure – itself, and in spite of the persistence of old favourites, new patterns constantly evolve, for fly-tiers are fortunately not inhibited by knowledge of what the fly looks like to the fish.

The Historical Background

CHAPTER ONE
FISHING FOR PLEASURE

As inward love breeds outward talk,
The hound some praise, and some the hawk,
Some, better pleas'd with private sport,
Use tennis, some a mistress court:
But these delights I neither wish,
Nor envy, while I freely fish.

The Angler's Song, IZAAK WALTON

Nine years ago a tumulus at Hochdorf near Stuttgart in West Germany was discovered to be the tomb of a Celtic chieftain. He was about six feet tall and had died at about the age of 40 in the mid-6th century BC. The treasures within the tomb included bronze couches, bronze cauldrons and gold jewellery, as well as more ephemeral items such as a birchbark hat and elaborate textiles. Among the dead chief's more mundane possessions were – iron fish hooks.

Hitherto the earliest North European finds of iron fish hooks had been in Norway and dated from about AD 400. It is not merely for the antiquity of the hooks, though, that this German find seems important. This was no humble labourer or servant: this was a chief. It seems unlikely that fishing was a necessity for a man of this importance. Surely, he must have been a fisherman for his own pleasure.

The first fish eaten by human beings were probably stranded by receding water, by chance or design. A close-packed rank of humans encircling the fish and driving them into the bank may have been the most practical form of fishing. The method is still in use off the Pacific islands. Warm water, sunshine, the company of friends: there is a lot of laughter and fun – and a touch of fear if a shark comes too close for comfort. But this is not yet fishing as a sport. Nets were probably used before hooks and lines, and nets may have derived from branches held in the water as a barrier.

Spears must have been an early item of tackle, developing rapidly into harpoons. Chemicals derived from plants are used by some of the people of the Amazon basin today, and the properties of some plants to deoxygenate water and thus knock out the fish may have been known for thousands of years.

Weirs and traps, developed centuries, even millennia ago, have hardly changed in some parts of the world. In tidal areas, where fish will run in high water, they can be impounded as the water drops, or may become stranded or easily accessible to spear or net. The few remaining commercial fishers in the Severn estuary still use primitive basket traps, known by such names as putchers, putts, cribs, hecks and crucks, which are arranged in ranks with their mouths facing the flow of the tide or current. The tighter the weave of the baskets, which were made from pliant twigs such as willow or hazel, the smaller the fish that could be trapped in them.

There may well be an element of enjoyment and satisfaction about these methods of

R.R. McIan Spearing Salmon (1848), a technique employing torch and leister (usually five-tined), known as 'burning the water'.

*'... *M*ark what flies on the water', a drawing by James Thorpe from an edition of* The Compleat Angler *(1925).*

catching fish, but nothing yet approaching sport, which is undertaken *primarily* for the pleasure of it.

HOOKS AND OTHER ANGLES

The use of a hook may be the key to this transition. The earliest hook may have been a gorge hook, now outlawed in every civilised place, which is swallowed lengthwise by the fish and, when tension is applied, jams crosswise in the gullet. A curved hook or 'angle', as it was once called, has the obvious advantage that it can take a firm hold before the fish actually swallows it.

The first 'angles' were probably made of thorns. Juniper is, or recently was, regarded as indispensable in Sweden when fishing for burbot.

Other materials were used in the Stone Age – stone, shell and bone, which was probably in use 20,000 years ago, about the time when our ancestors were painting the caves of Lascaux and Altamira.

The use of bone to make fish hooks may have had something to do with determining their shape – rounded because a cross-section of a large bone offers a round shape and a section would involve comparatively little work in making a hook with the requisite qualities of penetration and retention.

Barbs may have originated on spears – which are, in a sense, different from hooks only in that they are attached to a rigid staff rather than a flexible line. At any rate, the efficacy of a barb was recognised thousands of years ago. Perhaps barbs were first used on hooks to prevent a livebait escaping, but someone must soon have noticed that a fish did not throw a barbed hook as easily as an unbarbed one.

In the Middle East, metal hooks were in use thousands of years before the time of that Celtic chieftain of Hochdorf. Bronze hooks, with and without barbs, have been found dating back to about 6000 BC. Examples of eyed hooks have also been found in Mesopotamia, which makes it all the more amusing to read Victorian experts, like the great George Kelson (in *The Salmon Fly and How to Use It*), inveighing against 'new-fangled and useless' eyed hooks. The British Museum has hooks of Mycenaean make which are both eyed and barbed.

*T*itle page of the first
edition of
The Compleat Angler.

ANCIENT EGYPT AND CHINA

Nets, rods, lines and hooks feature in both the art and literature of ancient Egypt. Among a vast list of precepts of Ankhsheshnon in early demotic script, is this: *If a gardener becomes a fisherman, his trees perish.* A hint not to play truant, perhaps.

This does suggest that some Egyptians did really fish for the pleasure of fishing, even if fishing generally meant work, on the level of farming. Some Egyptians – if the Nubian Pharaoh Pinakhy, about 730 BC, can be taken as an example – considered fish to be impure food; those who had recently eaten fish were ritually defiled. However, fishing scenes, of netting and of rod and line fishing, were included in tomb paintings. Surely no Pharaoh, nor any of the aristocratic caste, would do so menial a job as fishing, either in his present world or the world to come, unless it were really a leisure activity, as dear to him, or nearly as dear, as hunting, which clearly was a favourite leisure occupation?

Paradoxically, hook-and-line fishing may have been a trade at this stage, restricted to commerce and the lower classes, while sport fishing was conducted with a spear or bow and arrow.

As we are often told, many technological developments took place in China long before Western civilisations achieved them and Ernest Schwiebert's monumental work *Trout* looks to the Far East for the origins of advanced fishing techniques. Among the examples he mentions are the use of cane rods and silk lines in the Chou Dynasty (1027–221 BC) and gold hooks, possibly tied with kingfisher feathers (a magic charm, perhaps, rather than a lure), described in the 'Chuh Tzu Manuscript'.

CLASSICAL TIMES

Homer has several brief references to fishing, but generally to net-fishing. No doubt warriors such as Agamemnon had the leisure time to fish for sport, if they wished, but there is no evidence that they did.

In general, classical references to fishing are few. Aristotle knew a great deal about fish, of course, including the fact that their scales indicate their age, but he has nothing to say about fishing. In classical literature fishermen are usually portrayed as very poor,

CHAPTER TWO
THE DEVELOPMENT OF TACKLE

*D*Opposite:
ean Wolstenholme
(1798–1882) Anglers
Playing their Catch in a
River Landscape.

over-worked, old, wrinkled and generally rather wretched. This can't have been good for the image of fishing as an upper-class sport.

Roman country gentlemen of the 1st century AD did like to go fishing although, if Pliny the Younger were typical, they did not take it very seriously. Pliny was able to cast a line into Lake Como from his window without the inconvenience of leaving his bed. His contemporary, Martial, was a keener fisherman, who used to put small fish back. It has been surmised that he used a jointed rod, though what pictorial evidence there is suggests that fishing rods were very short – hardly worth jointing. Still, one cannot interpret the evidence of, for instance, vase paintings, too literally.

One explanation of a love of fishing is that we are all still hunters at heart. The urge does not die when the need for food is satisfied; moreover, fishing, like hunting, is a means of achieving the satisfaction of doing a difficult thing well.

Most people who fish for sport probably form, if only in the back of their minds, their own version of such an idea – some more or less personal explanation of their interest. The mere catching of fish, alone, does not seem to constitute satisfaction. Nor does the efficacy of the method. On both counts there are other methods which, in terms of fish caught, would achieve more substantial results.

A fish which eats plant-life, or grubs along the bottom, is generally a less attractive quarry than a truly predatory fish and tends not to be favoured at the table; those of a predatory lifestyle are preferred. This is one way of making a distinction between gamefish, good to eat, attractive in habit and appearance, and coarse fish, less appetising and less attractive in 'personality'.

ESSENTIALS

The sport of fishing requires a fisherman who has the time to indulge in his pastime; a suitable fish for him to spend time trying to catch; a hook by which it may be held reasonably securely; a line fine enough not to frighten the fish yet not so fine as to break

A portrait of the contemplative angler, Izaak Walton, from a 19th-century edition of The Compleat Angler.

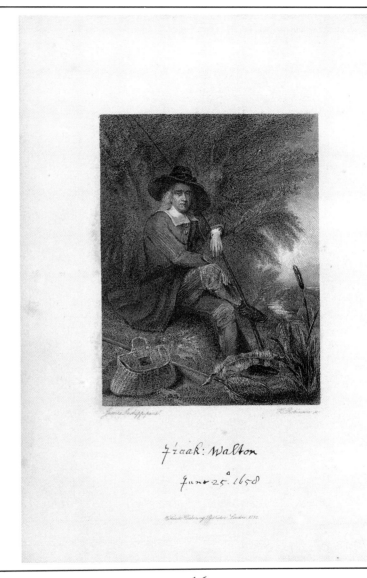

when it is hooked; and a rod capable of projecting the hook into the water and, when the fish is hooked, of providing shock absorption that prevents the line breaking.

Before reels were invented, the line was attached to the slender end of the rod, and recently there has been a resurgence of interest in the pole-fishing technique, never wholly abandoned by Thames roach fishermen, for taking small coarse fish. The technique is rarely used for gamefish, though deep-sea commercial tuna fishing is carried on even now with stout rods, fixed lines and barbless hooks.

Apart from the distance limit on casting, this method prevents a large fish running far without a break, and although line-winders were used before 1613, it must have been a great relief when reels, along with rod rings, came into general use.

A *Hardy 'Perfect', one of the most popular fly reels ever made, the first version of which was introduced in 1892.*

REELS

The early history of the reel is unknown. The Greeks, who had Archimedes screws in the early 3rd century BC, certainly had the technical know-how to make metal reels, but had little impulse to do so. The Chinese can probably claim to be the earliest users of a fishing reel. There is a painting dating from the Sung Dynasty (960–1280) which shows fishermen with reels on their rods, and Schwiebert mentions two other examples, a 12th-century painting by Ma Yuan called *Angler on a Wintry Lake*, and a 14th-century work by Wu Chen. These are much earlier than any known European reference.

The earliest mention of a 'winder' or reel in England occurs in Thomas Barker's *Art of Angling*, published in 1651 (two years before Walton's *Compleat Angler*). By the time of his second edition in 1657, he was able to describe a reel used for salmon. He also provided an illustration of this device, but unfortunately, as A. Courtney Williams remarked, it bears 'no resemblance to anything, unless it be to a plan for an outside closet'.

Early reels were made of brass. Wood was not widely used until the 19th century. This is curious, as wood might have been the better material given the state of precision engineering in the late 17th – early 18th centuries. Wooden reels were in fact widely used in Britain up to the middle of this century.

Henry Raeburn (1756–1823) Lt Col Bryce McMurdo. *This magnificent picture by one of the greatest British portrait painters has the added virtue of meticulous attention to details of salmon tackle.*

HOOKS AND WEIGHTS

The use of metal was certainly vital for the development of an efficient hook. Fishermen have always been, understandably, pernickety about hooks, and they still are today, in spite of the remarkable refinements and varieties introduced by hook manufacturers. Consider a hook manufacturing plant like Mustad's in Sweden. It is difficult not to be overwhelmed by their range of hook styles to suit fishing conditions all over the world: from sizes weighing over a pound each, which can take the largest sharks and other sea fish, to tiny freshwater hooks of which 1,000 weigh four grammes. Hurum (Mustad's official historian), writing in 1976, states that there was a time when 103,800 different types of hook were being manufactured.

An Egyptian illustration of hooks on sale in a market is datable to about the Sixth Dynasty and the ancient Greeks depicted fishing scenes with great delicacy and accuracy on their pottery. Thanks to Homer and exemplified by, for example, finds at Knossos from the late Minoan age (1425 BC), we know that the Greeks certainly had bronze if not iron fish hooks at that time, and judging by other surviving examples of their metalwork, they had the craftsmen to make hooks of a high standard.

Homer's mention of lead weights is the earliest reference I have found to the use of lead in fishing. However, a weight such as a split shot or its modern equivalent added somewhere on the leader is not so easily cast as a weighted fly. Lines themselves may incorporate weight, or be of different densities appropriate to the rate of sink required. Development in lines over the past two or three decades has greatly widened the scope of the fly-fisherman.

LINES

In fly casting the weight of the line activates the rod to produce the impulse that projects the fly across the water. A dense line has a small diameter and sinks quickly; a line which floats has less density and a larger diameter; even so, length for length, lines with the same rating correspond in weight. Thus a rod rated for a particular line weight will function well with lines of different density.

In the early days lines had to be made from any materials near to hand. The Chinese used silkworm gut as their fixed line, while other peoples used horsehair. This material was carefully chosen, preferably from the tail of a stallion as it would not be weakened by urine, and free of blemishes. It was in equal lengths so that each knotted section would be consistent within itself, and might taper down to a single hair. Knots in horsehair lines were whipped and waxed, but by about the middle of the 18th century, horsehair lines could be obtained which were plaited and knotless. Anyone who has ever used one of these lines will agree that they are more effective than they sound.

Materials such as horsehair decay, and therefore we have only the comments of angling authors to rely on for their use in earlier times. Standard recommendations for horsehair, no doubt unchanged for centuries, were repeated in Walton's *Compleat Angler*:

> Your hair should be round and clear, and free from galls, or scabs, or frets: for a well chosen, even, clear, round hair, of a kind of glass colour, will prove as strong as three uneven scabby hairs that are ill-chosen, and full of galls and uneveness . . . . let your hair be washed ere you go about to twist it; and then choose . . . . hairs that be of an equal bigness, for such do eventually stretch all together, and break all together, which hairs of an uneven bigness never do, but break singly . . . .

One of Walton's commentators, Andrew Lang (1896), suggests that Pepys was the first to write of the use of silkworm gut as a line for fishing. Both materials must be regarded as having the same virtues and failings: reasonably strong under a steadily applied pull, and much weaker against a sudden jolt. Varnished cat gut was used by some late 17th-century anglers but was not widely adopted. As soon as reels became current, lines could become longer than before. Knots became more of a nuisance and short lengths had to be woven or braided into a continuous whole. Combinations of materials were used, particularly silk and horsehair, though this was an unsatisfactory mixture as the two materials behave differently when wet, and all the strain falls on one or other. Silk lines proved highly practical after an oil impregnation process was developed, which gave a good surface finish and resistance to rot.

It may seem surprising that silk did not take over from horsehair more swiftly, but

Opposite:

The notion that fly-fishing for trout was an exclusively middle-class sport is incorrect for many parts of England (and all of Scotland). This fly fisherman of about 1857 has a long rod and no reel.

Workers making silkworm gut in a Spanish factory about 1897. The product was purchased by Hardy Bros.

its advantages, in the context of time, were less than might be supposed. The early silk lines were of course nothing like the fly fisherman's line of modern times, being light, undressed, apt to tangle at the slightest provocation and prone to rot. It was not conservatism alone, admittedly a powerful factor in the evolution of fishing tackle, which made anglers prefer horsehair, always provided they could obtain it in that desirable glass colour, even and round. Moreover, woven hair lines, which frequently featured in the advertisements of late 18th-century tackle dealers, were an improvement on the knotted kind, despite some loss of strength. Tackle dealers also sold a great variety of ingenious 'engines' for twisting horsehair, and many exotic recipes were recommended for dyeing lines.

By about 1800 it was possible to buy lines of woven silk which 'run taper like the lash of a coach whip', but horsehair was still more common in fly-fishing as well as other branches of angling. Leaders were frequently made of silkworm gut, but in the north of England, where the average size of trout was smaller, horsehair remained popular throughout the 19th century. Expert anglers used a single hair next to the fly, which demanded a gentle touch with a large fish.

Maintenance of silk lines was important, but since the 1950s nylon and dacron braids have superseded silk, and plastic coatings have been developed which give flexibility plus resistance to surface wear. These coatings control the density of the line, and line weights to accord with rod designs – AFTM weight or ratings – have become internationally standardised and consistent.

"HOLDFAST" SEA LINES.

CHAPTER THREE

THE DEVELOPMENT OF FLY-FISHING

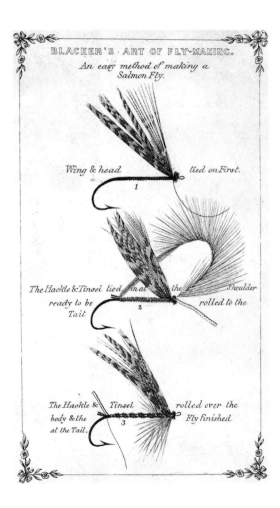

Hooks, lines, rods and reels have been in use since early times and of course they have altered beyond recognition, yet there has been little development in their principles. New materials, from time to time, have added extra efficiency. On the basis of this tackle – simple in principle though by no means unsophisticated – a philosophy of recreational fishing has developed, wide and liberal in its approach. At its pinnacle is the sport of fly-fishing.

In English there is an early manuscript, the *Treatyse of Fysshinge wyth an Angle*, which dates from the early 15th century and was printed in 1496, which encapsulates the idea that fishing can take its place with credit among sports such as hunting, fowling and falconry as a pleasurable pastime, therapeutic and contemplative. The work is broad-ranging, being a mixture of technique, description and philosophy. Rod-making, choice of line, hook-making – all these technical matters are discussed – but perhaps its most interesting feature is the fly patterns it presents. From this moment we embark upon the concept of fly fishing as we know it today, although there are tantalising hints of its practice at a much earlier period.

THE FIRST ARTIFICIAL?

The first unequivocal step towards fly-fishing is found in the writings of Aelian, a Roman of the third century AD. He wrote of a river called the Astraeus, flowing between the cities of Beroea and Thessalonika (nowadays Verroia and Salonika). Translation gives 'spotted fishes' for his words. From his description, they were trout; and their behaviour, which he also describes, we can recognise as typical trout behaviour. The fly, he suggests, was made of red wool and feathers from below the wattles of a cock.

I envisage the early fly-tier of that period as being a nomad shepherd with a craft tradition of rugmaking. What Aelian does not say is whether the fly is made as a specific imitation in colour and shape of the *hipporus*, the natural fly the fish are taking, or whether it is more of a lure, dressed from materials to hand, and the red used to provoke the predatory character of the fish. Whereas the *Treatyse* is specific about its dressings and about the natural flies which were to be imitated month by month, the

(12)

Daw ruff or Tom Titt Tail Silk Lead or Darke purple coulor with a little Moules furr for Bodey If you wing it take the Tom Titt tail and a small Cock or Hen Hackle the coulor of of straw for legs No. 0 or 1 for Hook The Wings are a verry Darke Blue the coulor of New Garth Iorn—the Bodey of a Darke bluey Durty Drab with six leggs of a straw Coulor— the Head of a Darke reddy Coulor to be fished one point and one Top anger.

2nd Edition of his book on angling, three pages of as nicely written fly fishing matter as ever were penned! The Jenny Spinner. The transformation of this fly appears to have been unobserved or not cared for by the Author, nevertheless it is a most beautiful, delicate and deadly killing fly. A pattern is here-after given. The Nuthatch and the *Cock* Merlin Hawk have both good feathers for the wings of the Iron blue; but perhaps no better feathers can be used than the dark blue ones from the breast of a well plumaged Waterhen, two tips of which make first-rate wings. The *Hen* Merlin is double the size of the cock, of a different colour, and affords no feathers for this fly.—ED.

hipporus of Aelian suggests a composite. Since *hippos* is Greek for horse, it would be pleasing if this were a pun on horsefly, but Aelian writes amply about gadflies and horseflies elsewhere.

The *Treatyse* was written before flies had Linnaean classifications, but several can be identified. J. W. Hills, the historian of fly-fishing, claimed to have identified all but one, though other experts are more doubtful. The list probably represents a standard set, evolved over a long period, and it was a long time before any substantial advance was made over the flies listed in the *Treatyse*.

AN EARLY SPANISH ENTOMOLOGIST

The next stage comes in a remarkable Spanish work, the *Manuscript of Astorga* by Juan de Bergera, written in 1624. At that time Astorga was an important town in the north of Spain. He is assumed to have been a writer rather than a fisher, because the text admits that he compiled the work, the documents from which it was drawn having the approval of anglers of great experience. The book is concerned with the tying and dressing of feathers in order to fish for trout, and there is enough in the text to suggest that some of the flies might have been tied to float.

Although the manuscript was lost in a fire, a facsimile was published by Preben Torp Jacobsen, bound together with modern Spanish, French and English versions. Twenty-four patterns are illustrated in this reprint. I fished near Santander some years ago, long before I was aware of De Bergera, and bought local trout flies. If I compare style of body and hackle placement, Spain was quite remarkably advanced in 1624 and things have not changed much since. Even Cotton, whose addition on fly-fishing to *The Compleat Angler* in 1676 was a huge advance on the *Treatyse*, was not as sophisticated as the Spaniard.

Cotton gave us the concept of 'fine and far off', but he appears to consider that fly-fishing is simply a matter of casting with the wind and letting the flies drift round at the whim of the current.

The "Halford 1904 Series" Dry Fly Boxes.
(1913 MODELS.)

No. 1.

MAY FLY BOX.

Size 5½ × 3½ ins.
× ⅞ ins.

PRICE 10/6.

No. 2.

SMALL FLY BOX.

Size 5½ × 3½ ins.
× 1¼ ins.

PRICE 25/-.

DUPLICATING COTTON

Since they are the only evidence we have, it is natural that readers and even historical researchers place great faith in what they read in books. But books inevitably tell only part of the story, and in particular, they do not tell us things which, though we may be ignorant of them, were common knowledge for contemporary readers. Thus, if I say I am going to Birmingham, it will probably be assumed that I am going by car, as I do not say expressly that I shall take the train or the bus. Similarly, if we read in an old book of 'floating' flies, we tend to think of a dry fly perched above the water, a concept almost certainly unknown until the 18th century.

There have been rather few attempts to duplicate the tackle and technique of 17th-century anglers in order to find out how they actually worked, but one such experiment was carried out by the well-known British angler, Conrad Voss Bark. He used a 17 ft 6 in hazel rod and a line of plaited horsehair links 22 ft long. He found that the line could be cast easily across a moderate wind and with some difficulty against it, though when the wind freshened a little he could get nowhere. The horsehair line proved almost impossible to sink and a wet fly would work just below the surface. A dry fly of modern type, when rubbed with mutton fat, floated quite naturally.

THE DRY FLY – DEFINITE NEWS!

The floating fly as we know it is usually dated to Pulman's *Vade Mecum of Fly-Fishing*. His first edition of 1841 gives the first statement of an intention to fish a dry fly in the manner in which we nowadays interpret this style of fishing. It is more than a note on a floating fly. In his third edition (1851), Pulman adds a word or two about false casting, generally considered a crucial step in the evolution of fly fishing. Stoddart, a redoubtable expert on the Tweed and its tributaries, also mentioned the subject in his *Angler's Companion* (2nd ed., 1853):

> It is not an unusual practice, on recovering the line, and before recasting, to describe a figure of eight, twice or thrice successively, in the air with the fly-cast, in order to relieve the plumage of the hooks of the moisture imbibed.

A *page from Herbert Maxwell's edition of Ronalds's* The Fly Fisher's Entomology *(1913) which contained actual flies.*

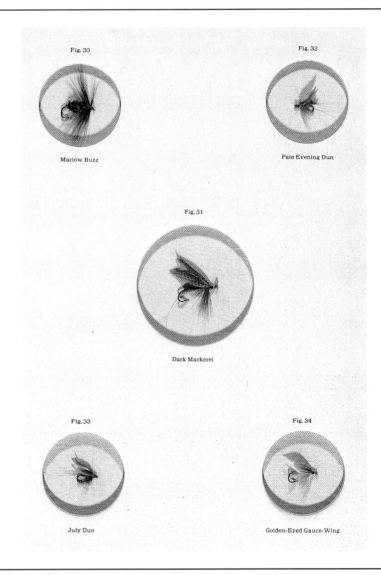

Fig. 30

Marlow Buzz

Fig. 32

Pale Evening Dun

Fig. 31

Dark Mackerel

Fig. 33

July Dun

Fig. 34

Golden-Eyed Gauze-Wing

IMITATING NATURE

Entomology had not failed to keep up with other developments. Richard Bowlker in *The Art of Angling Improved* (1747) and more especially his son Charles, who brought out a second edition in 1774, vastly enlarged the range of fly patterns, though it was Alfred Ronalds who in *The Fly Fisher's Entomology* (1836) set up a workable set of parallels between the naturals and the artificials that imitate them. Later editions of *The Fly-Fisher's Entomology* contained 49 flies – with one drawing for the natural and one for its corresponding artificial – and gave them their scientific names. The Linnaen nomenclature had been established for some 100 years, yet Ronalds was the first to classify the trout fisherman's flies scientifically.

Let us stand back for a moment, and see how far we have progressed. We know which insects are which, and how they may be tied. We can fish below the surface, and tackle permits us to cast a fair distance in favourable conditions. We know we can fish on the surface, but we are short of a good handbook on fishing a dry fly, a style so suited to the relatively slow-fishing chalk streams of Hampshire and Wiltshire.

DRY-FLY PURISM

Francis Francis, in a magazine article, explained how effective the dry fly was for him on the River Itchen. But it was Halford who formulated the code of the dry fly. His books of the 1880s were regarded as so dogmatic by some of his contemporaries that the most unfisherman-like acrimony resulted. Halford was interpreted as saying that the only proper way to fish for trout was with a dry fly: a trout had to be observed feeding, that trout specifically was to be fished for, with an exact imitation of the insect on which it was feeding. Any other procedure was, implicitly, beneath the notice of true sportsmen.

Anyone who takes the trouble to read Halford now – and it's a worthwhile occupation – will be surprised to find that in print he is nowhere near as dogmatic as his reputation. The whole dry-fly controversy was largely created by his followers, who regarded him much as the ancient Hebrews regarded Moses.

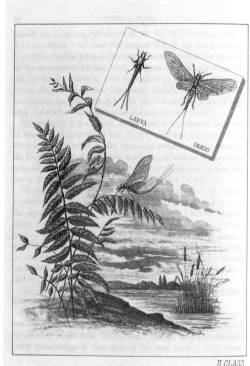

LARVA

IMAGO

DRAKES

II CLASS

Alfred de Bréanski

Left:
Alfred de Breanski The Lledr Valley above Bettws y Coed. *A tributary of the Conway, the Lledr's main reputation is for autumn salmon and sewin (sea trout).*

Halford's fly-fishing career began on the Wandle, where local experts advised him to 'fish dry'. The flies supplied to him by local dealers bore no resemblance to natural insects, but he did well enough with them until he came to fish the Test, where he came to the conclusion that it was necessary to study the habits of the fish and the nature of the insects on which they feed.

Halford was a man of considerable intellectual power, and he made himself an expert on everything connected with trout and the fly. His association with dry-fly purism and the conflict with G.E.M. Skues, apostle of the nymph, caused him to be under-valued at one time, but he remains, as a current Test expert, David Jacques, has said, 'a great man to whom we all owe a monument of everlasting gratitude.'

Since Halford and Skues there has been little that is really new, simply refinements of detail and developments in materials and time and again the rediscovery of old truths that have been forgotten by all but the oldest and best-read anglers.

CHAPTER FOUR
MODERN FLY-FISHING

One of the joys of the fisherman is his tackle, and nothing will ever stop him seeking improvements and accessories – regardless (I suspect) of their effectiveness. As I have said before, catching fish is by no means the only consideration in the sport of fishing.

By the last quarter of the 19th century, virtually all our fly-fishing tackle and techniques were established in familiar form. Since then there has been much modernisation, especially in the use of artificial materials, but little really fundamental change.

RODS

In the days of Halford on the clear chalk streams of southern England an ideal rod for dry-fly fishing was made of cane and was about 11–12 feet long. Greenheart, the other rod material then in favour, produced a lazy, slow action, bending right down to the butt, and was more suitable for wet-fly fishing. Whole cane had been used by the ancient Chinese, and is to be seen throughout the world to this day, but since it is the outer part of the cane which contains the hardest, most close-packed fibres, a split- or built-cane rod makes a more precise instrument. 'Split' cane is the slivers from this outer part, triangular in section, which are glued and bound together. If the taper of these long slivers is the result of calculation and design, then a series of rods may have different flexing characteristics or, as fishermen say, different 'actions'.

Pulman wrote about the need to dry the line by false casting: slow-actioned rods do this less well than fast-actioned ones. A fast action not only shakes water off a fly better than a slower, it makes presentation of a dry fly easier and more precise.

Although in 1922 Hardy Bros made up a rod from cane grown in Devon which seemed quite as good as any rod made from foreign bamboo, the most sought-after material was the best *Arundaria amabilis* from China, which has the finest qualities for cane rod construction.

For a long time split cane was the supreme material for rods – hexagonal, double-built, steel-centred, hollow-built, etc. – but the best material was expensive and difficult to obtain.

The first artificial material to have any success was steel tube. Some good spinning rods were made of steel, not the least of their virtues being their virtual indestructibility, but the real revolution came with glass fibre. This had lightness and strength, and above all it was cheap, whether made as a tapered tube or solid.

Light as it is, glass fibre is still heavy in comparison with more modern materials such as carbon fibre (graphite) and boron, but these are more expensive, so glass rods are still available – and do sterling duty. Cane is still favoured by some for its feel and character, but Hardy Bros in Pall Mall say that they sell scarcely one split-cane rod (hand-made and therefore expensive) to 200 carbon rods.

Weight is naturally an important factor in rod length, which in turn has an important effect on casting. Rods grew shorter when lines were improved, enabling fishermen to cast the same, or a greater, distance with less effort. The addition of a few ounces may not seem much, but over a long day's fishing it can make an enormous difference.

However, a long rod has many obvious benefits. It is easier, with a comparatively

LNER **WESTERN HIGHLANDS** LMS

IT'S QUICKER BY RAIL

FULL INFORMATION FROM LNER AND LMS OFFICES AND AGENCIES

Old reels. The top one bears an inscription and the date 1898.

long rod, to control the line on the water and to clear obstacles on the back cast, and today the wheel has almost turned full circle. Long rods as advocated in earlier times are returning to favour, though now with the benefit of extremely efficient low-friction lines and much lighter rod-building materials.

REELS

The essence of a 'wheel', 'wynch' or reel, has not changed: it is a reservoir for line, fitted with a check to prevent over-runs and put extra strain on a running fish. Multipliers, in which one rotation of the handle produces more than one rotation of the spool, are not new, and are a ready option even if they impose a slight penalty in weight. However, if rods could be made lighter, then so could reels. Brass is many times heavier than, for example, aluminium or magnesium. Reel makers have worked steadily in composite materials and alloys, refining, lightening and improving reliability. The search for weight-reduction has led to reels made in plastic and carbon fibre.

Wood has taken a long time to die out as a material for reels. Walnut and brass are the usual components of the old starback, and trout reels of that type were certainly in use as recently as the 1920s. At least they were attached to the rod. In Scrope's *Days and Nights of Salmon Fishing on the Tweed* (1843) the pirn (an old Scottish name for a reel) was strapped to a belt round the waist: reasonable enough for casting, but what happens when the angler hooks 'a lusty fellow, strong as an elephant, swift as a thunderbolt'?

LINES AND LEADERS

Fly lines, from being horsehair, silk and horsehair, and eventually oil-dressed silk, have settled down to a regular formula. The core is a tightly woven synthetic material such as dacron, with a limited amount of stretch. Bonded to this core, and with similar stretch characteristics, is PVC, or some formula of plastic of differing densities. Lines with the broadest diameter and least density float, while the thinnest and densest sink more quickly. The line surface is designed to be as smooth and supple as possible, and the line shape – its taper – is a matter of precise calculation. Much depends on the match of rod and line. When they are well-matched the distance, depth and speed at which the fly can be fished can all be controlled. Ill-matched, and some of these qualities will be lost.

The best gut leaders were strong, supple and fine in diameter in relation to their breaking strain, but they had two drawbacks. First, since the silkworm could produce only short lengths, leaders had to be knotted. Second, they had to be thoroughly soaked, before fishing began, to make them supple. A substitute which had all the good qualities of gut without its drawbacks was not easily found, and nylon leaders did not come into general use until after the Second World War. They were not the perfect solution either. Although the new material did not need presoaking, it was more slippery than gut and demanded a new repertoire of knots. However, it provided great strength for equivalent diameter and, of course, it could be made in unlimited lengths.

Leaders may be straight lengths of constant breaking strain, or they may be tapered to a fine point. They may be braided, and some are braided with a metallic element to assist sinking, but the principle remains of a fine, strong and as nearly as possible invisible connection between fly and line.

*S*almon flies, from Farlow's catalogue (about 1910).

FLIES

Flies have changed in detail but not really in principle. Metallic flashes can be used either as a body material or in strands as part of the wing; plastics are moulded to form body shapes; and new natural materials such as deer hair, which must nevertheless have an untraceably long history with the American Indians, have found favour in the form of the Muddler Minnow and its derivatives.

Although line and lead have been incorporated into the bodies of flies to add weight when required, nowadays the choice of hook can be made from a wide selection. The modern range of hooks, so carefully based on experiment and design, the almost limitless variety of bends, points, barbs, length of shank, width of gape, weight of wire, etc., would have astonished the author of the 15th-century *Treatyse*, whose hooks were probably formed from bent needles.

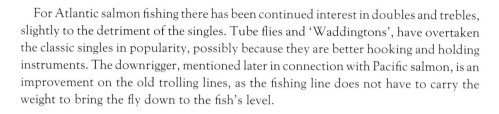

*Brook Trout Fishing –
'An Anxious Moment', a
Currier and Ives print (1862).
Alas, the landing net has
been left behind.*

For Atlantic salmon fishing there has been continued interest in doubles and trebles, slightly to the detriment of the singles. Tube flies and 'Waddingtons', have overtaken the classic singles in popularity, possibly because they are better hooking and holding instruments. The downrigger, mentioned later in connection with Pacific salmon, is an improvement on the old trolling lines, as the fishing line does not have to carry the weight to bring the fly down to the fish's level.

HI-TECH

Electronic aids, such as depth finders, help to locate schools of fish and to determine their depth. One enterprising fisherman set up remote-control television to see how chinook salmon were reacting to his trolling baits. Lake fishermen discuss their methods and catches with colleagues in other boats by means of Citizen's Band radio. There are no doubt more innovations to come in fishing electronics, but how 'fair' their use may be is open to question. They are scarcely essential aids, in any case.

BALANCED TACKLE

Since fly-fishing depends upon the weight of the line rather than on the weight of the bait or fly, it follows that if the fly weighs too much it will put the fly-rod out of balance. At the other end of the scale, the wire of very small hooks will pull out straight if line, leader and rod are too hefty.

General-purpose rods for trout are between eight and nine foot long and take a number 6 line. This allows for a wide range of fly sizes in all reasonable weathers; it allows the delivery of the fly to effective distances without superhuman techniques; and the tackle is not so heavy that a day's fishing becomes unduly exhausting. For fishing the clearest streams in the brightest weather for the shyest and most sophisticated trout, a rod which takes a 1 or 2 line may be chosen, but its performance will be badly affected by a strong wind, and whatever the conditions the angler will need a gentle hand in playing his fish when the leader has a breaking strain perhaps as low as one pound.

In general, sportsmanship dictates that tackle should be no finer than it need be, for fear of breaks. A fisherman earns no credit for leaving a fish in the water with a hook fixed in its jaws. If the plan is to release the fish after it has been caught, an extended period of play may result in such fatigue that the fish does not recover. Too fine tackle defeats the purpose of the exercise. It remains undisputed, however, that intelligent application of fine tackle may prove a help in a knotty fishing problem – when wise fish are taking minute food items in clear water and difficult light. Tackle that is too strong will make the fish suspicious.

Salmon-fishing tackle should be chosen with equal precision. Many salmon rivers are big enough to call for a long, two-handed rod. Length of rod is valuable not only for the obvious reason of projecting the fly a greater distance, but more importantly, in helping to control the line in or on the water. A long rod permits an easy pick-up of a good length of line and redirects it back over the river with a minimum of effort. Strength and power are important when fishing a heavy line with a big, heavy fly; delicacy and nicety of presentation are important on clear summer days. This does not mean a *shorter* rod is then called for – merely a *lighter* rod, for line control (which influences the pace of the fly) is still necessary. The principle of fishing no finer than necessary applies, and a line with a six- or seven-pound breaking strain is handled very satisfactorily by a light, two-handed rod without the need for a single-hander.

On many rivers there is much to be said against a single-hander. Far more false casting is necessary to achieve reasonable line lengths when the background precludes overhead casting, and line control is harder. In 'heavy' conditions, however heavy and strong the rod, there is a limit to the size and weight of fly which can be cast without hazard to the angler.

The competent two-handed rod fisherman spends more of his time actually fishing than a single-hander, because his fly lifts and lands again more swiftly, while the hard-working single-hander is making half a dozen false casts to extend his line.

It is worth making an effort, by instruction and practice, to improve one's casting. The ability to cast well is in itself a supremely satisfying exercise and it has an immense influence on results. Now, good instructional videos are easily available which teach both casting and fishing and help to give a more balanced understanding.

Opposite:
*L*ionel Edwards (1878–1966) Going for a 'John MacNab'.

Varieties of Game Fish

John Russell Castle
Grant Water: River Spey,
(about 1870). Russell
specialised in this subject and
no artist has painted salmon
with greater devotion.

O Sir, doubt not but that Angling is an art: is it not an art to deceive a Trout with an artificial Fly? a Trout that is more sharp-sighted than any Hawk you have named, and more watchful and timorous than your high-mettled Merlin is bold?

The Compleat Angler, Izaak Walton

INTRODUCTION

There is really no such thing as a mystique of fly-fishing: it's a practical business which encompasses a huge choice of manner, style and approach to delight its participants.

Most fly-fishermen are no longer hunting for food from need, though one may slip down to the loch for half an hour in the evening to see if there is a trout for supper, but for the excitement of the challenge, and the allure of achieving a particular goal in a manner requiring a range of expertise (and luck).

The *Salmonidae* are a diverse race, some very localised, some widely spread. Since the means of transporting ova was discovered, just before the turn of the century, some species have proved excellent colonisers. Providing they were introduced to water systems which were free from pollution and extremes of temperature, and had sufficient food supply, the imports thrived. Brown trout and rainbow trout now inhabit both hemispheres, though the one sprang from Europe and the other from North America.

All trout and salmon are handsome fish, of elegant streamlined shape, delivering power and energy, and with few exceptions they are excellent eating. Not only are they tasty, they are nourishing (one diet sheet has claimed that fresh salmon is cheaper than cod, as it has four times more nutritive value and yet is less than four times more expensive). Finally, the temperate zones in which the fish thrive offer some of the finest scenery for souls jaded by the pressures of urbanisation.

The customary angling term for all trout and salmon species is 'game fish', but other species which have similar qualities and are similarly fished for can be drawn into this category. For keen fly-fishers, all fish which will take a fly are game fish.

SALMON TROUT (VAR.)

CHAPTER ONE
BROWN TROUT

The Queen Mother fishing in 1927.

Our more detailed look at the game fish will start with trout, for they are the fly fisherman's most common quarry.

The trout's importance comes from its present wide availability. The brown trout, *Salmo trutta*, is essentially a European creature, its original habitat extending from the Mediterranean basin (which includes Asia Minor) northwards to the Arctic Circle. At one stage, every possible detectable variation entitled a fish to the status of a species. Plates in old fishing books identify any number of long-discredited examples. Now, generally, scientists have come to describe the fish as 'polytypic': there is but one brown trout. Nevertheless, it includes two creatures of very different habits. In one form it is resident in rivers and lakes; in the other it migrates to the sea for rich feeding, before returning, like the salmon, to the river of its birth to spawn. This is the sea-trout.

There has been massive interest in the genetics of trout. To rear them for table consumption most efficiently, with optimised growth rate and maximum freedom from disease, scientists are taking a look at the chromosome differences. Perhaps there will be a reclassification after all, one which will support Highland Scots in their claim that *their* brown trout is certainly not the same as the southern brown trout.

It would be nice to think that our next cast might produce a forty-pounder. Brown trout can achieve this sort of weight: the deep Swiss lakes attest to it, and the White River in Arkansas has the finest modern record for trophy fish of over 20 lb, an occasional example weighing over 30 lb. A fish cannot achieve this sort of size without ideal conditions of temperature, food and security. The White River is rich both in insect forms for the trout's early development, and in more substantial forage when the trout requires a bigger menu. The waters of Peru and Argentina also exemplify this rapid growth, with 20-pounders not rare and double-figure trophies commonplace.

Both these are examples of colonisation, where man has introduced a successful species to a niche otherwise unexploited. Australia and New Zealand were similarly colonised in the 19th century, and the growth rates of the trout soon after their establishment were amazing. *Angling in New Zealand* (1924), claims growth rates of from one pound to three pounds a year, and within a few years fish of an exceptional size were captured. Twenty and 30-pounders are well authenticated, and there is a tale of a 40-pounder from Lake Coleridge, near Canterbury. It was not uncommon once

COMMON TROUT.

for one man to catch over 100 lb weight in a day. Sizes have diminished nowadays with, for example, Taupo fish averaging 4–5 lb. Rainbows are more common than browns.

NORTH AMERICA

In North America, the brook trout (*Salvelinus fontinalis*), which actually belongs to the char family, bore the brunt of the introduction of the brown, for the brown trout has come to take a share in the habitat. Brookies are comparatively short-lived, and they thrive in colder waters. When massive timber stands were reduced for lumber, one effect was a rise in river temperatures. This suited brown trout, but the native brook trout diminished.

Fly-fishing in North America naturally predated the introduction of brown trout by two or three generations. American fly-fishers could hardly have failed to realise that what worked in British or Irish waters was not necessarily ideal on Appalachian streams. In a note on fly-fishing in his edition of *The Compleat Angler*, published in 1847, George Washington Bethune (one of that numerous tribe of angling clerics) observed that trout in many American streams were less sophisticated than their British cousins. In those days, of course, it was still possible to cast an artificial fly to a trout which had never seen such a thing before, but as Bethune pointed out, 'directions serviceable in Great Britain and Ireland, must be greatly modified to be of use among us . . .'

Brown trout brought with them in the 1880s a whole new culture of fishing. The generations of fishing Americans had developed a very satisfactory fishing system – downstream wet, with lure-type flies – for brook trout and black bass, which was less successful for the browns. It was as if the browns had read the British fishing books and had taught themselves to be selective in their new home.

Brookies had a reputation for being willing strikers; browns were too particular to take just any offering. So works such as Halford's were widely studied, and a parallel but different American dry-fly culture grew apace. If fishing has a mystical aspect, it is surely related to the whims and caprices of the brown trout with their tremendous selectivity among food forms (and appropriate imitations).

The challenge to meet the problems posed by the fish has stimulated the intellectual

Winslow Homer
watercolour
(late 19th century).

and analytical approach to fly fishing which, to so many enthusiasts, is its greatest charm. American fishers at first condemned the browns for their unwillingness to play their part in the sport, but soon rethought their tactics, devising their own imitations or representations (not exact imitations) of the different and much more varied insects to be seen on American streams, and produced a reasonable response from the fish. The two trout-fishing cultures – British and American – still dominate techniques world-wide, though practices in New Zealand and Australia, honed by a century of use, are now being introduced to Britain, particularly in the pursuit of trout in stillwater.

INFINITE VARIETY

The brown trout may not be the commonest of the trouts but it encompasses a great variety of types and habits. I have noted above that there are considerable differences among fish classified as brown trout. Even scientists accept that the local environment permits slight adaptations of colouring or other features. A fish in a clear, sandy-bottomed stream will be more lightly pigmented than the inhabitant of a dark, peaty loch. However, remove either trout from its native surroundings and it will soon accommodate itself to its new habitat. After a generation or so its descendants will show little evidence of foreign influence.

This is not to say that there are not 'races' of brown trout. An obvious example is the Loch Leven trout, which seems to have strong and persistent genetic traits. When a race is left isolated sufficiently long, its adaptation to its habitat becomes so ingrained that it can reasonably be considered as another species.

The evolution of the brown trout has been attributed partly to the exigencies of the ice ages, and whatever the truth of that, it has become a species of infinite variety. There is, for example, the marbled trout of southern Europe, particularly Yugoslavia; the Black Sea trout; the North African trout; and the Aral trout. All these are considered to be sub-species of the brown trout.

Evolution has produced in the Kura strain of the Caspian trout a fish which spawns only once, and can grow to the incredible weight of 112 lb. There is another subspecies which is restricted to Lake Garda in Italy. In Bulgaria I was told firmly that there was a

Opposite
Robin Armstrong A
Difficult Cast (detail)
(1989).

HANDY POCKET " PRIEST," DISGORGER, &c.

(Registered No. 543,931.)

FULL SIZE.

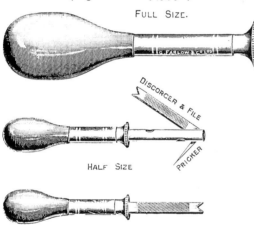

DISGORGER & FILE

HALF SIZE.

PRICKER

Farlow's combined
pocket priest and disgorger
(about 1908).

Balkan trout, but caught only rainbows and browns. The browns had rather few, large, dark spots on a slightly olive background. Balkan trout? Maybe.

In Ireland you may encounter a trout termed gillaroo. It was classified once as *stomatichus*, a reference to the very stout lining of its stomach developed to deal with its preferred diet of freshwater snails. T.C. Kingsmill Moore called it the panther of the water, the loveliest of all fish, thickly and profusely coloured and spotted on a satinwood background. He caught them up to 3 lb, though he was sure that they ran bigger. The gillaroo is nevertheless a brown trout.

The sonaghan or sonahan, a sober-looking fish coloured olive and iron grey with black spots, seems to be quite different in its liking for deep water, its small size (seldom over 1 lb), and its tendency to live in small shoals.

The ordinary brown is also distinguished from *Salmo ferox* – the fierce and rapacious trout, the great lake trout (known also to the Irish as buddagh), which flourishes on a diet of small fish. It is found in the deepest parts of natural stillwaters and can attain great weights.

S. ferox, however, can scarcely be classed as even a subspecies. Its size results merely from its adoption of a more nourishing diet than insects. Nonetheless, in England and Scotland the description 'ferox' is still often heard. I delight in the mystery of these mighty trout of possibly immense weights, tempted by morsels such as trolled half- or three-quarter-pound trout. 'Ferox' carries the same sort of frisson as the great white shark, or giant pike. We may surely continue to use the word as a description of a genuine type, whatever biologists may say.

There are illustrations of trout to be found captioned *nigripinnis*. Wales is often quoted as the birthplace of these trout, which have dark or almost black fins and tail, and achieve a maximum length of about 16 in. I mention it because there is no reason why trout should not be *described* for their differences. Part of the enjoyment of fishing is a study of the fish themselves, an appreciation of their form and colouring and markings, and we need some names, scientifically approved or not, for those interesting variations.

Robin Armstrong

CHAPTER TWO

CHAR

The colouration of trout is usually a pale background with a profusion of darker spots or freckles. The chars have a dark background, and the markings show paler against it. The leading edges of lower fins tend to be white, and the scales are smaller and more numerous. A point appreciable to my senses, though I have not seen it noted by other writers, is that char (like grayling) smell quite different from trout – a sort of cucumber smell (the grayling is always said to smell of wild thyme).

I was fishing a small lake in Wales which is stocked with brook trout when I first became aware of this – two little fish lying on the bottom boards of the boat and caught from the edge of the shadows as the sun slipped over the hills. These were certainly no trout, and my nose confirmed the opinion of my eye.

CHAR CHARACTERISTICS

The biologist distinguishes the char *Salvelinus* from the trout and salmon family *Salmo* largely by dentition and bone structure. Char are believed to have split fairly early from the salmonid stem. Like the brown trout, the char can show marked sexual dimorphism, with the males attaining more vivid markings at the approach of spawning maturity and developing a kype – an upward-projecting hook on the lower jaw. The Arctic char in particular can achieve brilliant crimson colouring, and it is little wonder that the Welsh call them *torgoch* ('red belly').

The char is an Ice Age relict, isolated sufficiently long to attain unchanging characteristics. In the British Isles we have several supposed 'species', but it is neater to consider them landlocked forms of the anadromous Arctic char, *Salvelinus alpinus*. Nevertheless, the char in Lake Windermere, for instance, have disparate characteristics: some breed in the Autumn and some in the Spring.

ARCTIC CHAR AND DOLLY VARDEN

The main interest of fishermen is devoted to the Arctic char in its two forms (land-locked and migratory); the brook trout, *S. fontinalis*; and the lake trout, *S. namaycush*. The vernacular names of these so-called trout spring from inexact usage. The early

1. WINDERMERE CHARR.   2. COLE'S CHARR.   3. GRAY'S CHARR.

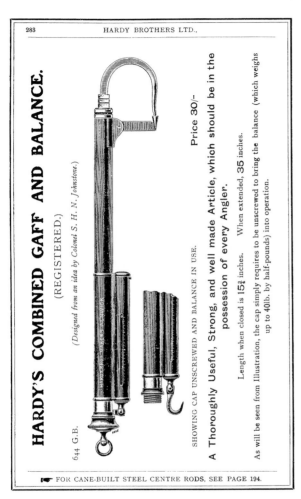

colonists noted the similarity of these native American fish to the brown trout of Europe. Those found in rivers were named according to their habit, as were the fish found in the lakes, though neither really is a trout.

The Arctic char and the brook trout may look quite similar. Arctic char do not have vermiculations on the back, nor do they have spotted back fins and tail fins. The tail fin is more forked than that of the brook trout, whose soubriquet 'square-tail' derives from this feature.

When a name for a fish has come into easily accepted use over many years it is upsetting to be told by fish experts that it does not qualify as a separate species. Such seems to be the case of the Dolly Varden, *S. malma* or *S. spectabilis*, or Western brook trout, which is currently having its species status scrutinised. Its differences from the Arctic char are admittedly so hard to determine that the two species may reasonably be considered to be one.

Larger examples of Dolly Varden are now called bull trout, on grounds of differences in the bones of the skull. The confusion is such, with habitat overlap, that the International Game Fish Association recommends record claimants to deep-freeze their catch for positive identification. At present, the record Arctic char is 29 lb 11 oz, Dolly Varden is 3 lb 13 oz, and bull trout 32 lb.

The life style of the Dolly Varden is highly predatory. It is not well regarded among sport fishermen as it is believed to take a toll on the young of preferred species such as steelhead, coho, and chinook. But there is no gainsaying its spirit when fresh from the sea, or in peak condition in fresh water.

The migratory Arctic char is silvery on entering the rivers. The males take on the intense crimson of their spawning livery to a greater extent than do the females, but they are at their best when they are freshest into the rivers. Their enthusiasm for taking a deep bait or fly is also greater at that time. At their best they are the fastest and strongest, size for size, of any of the salmonid game fish, although not great leapers when hooked.

Opposite:
Benjamin William Leader Derwentwater (1868), the home of the vendace.

Opposite:
Ogden *Pleissner* Along
the Granite Cliff, Moise
River, Quebec *(mid 1950s).*

BRITISH CHAR

It is quite an adventure to fish as far north as the rivers frequented by these fish, and the more usual quarry is the landlocked form under one of its many names. Without the sea diet their weight is usually small compared with their sea-run counterparts, which regularly achieve double-figures. In Britain fish over three quarters of a pound are larger than the norm, though fish of over two pounds are likely in deep lochs where trout are reared in cages. Enhanced feeding near the rearing cages produces some really outsize char trophies.

Char are particularly sensitive to environmental conditions: they thrive in cold waters and die if the temperature rises appreciably. Deep-feeders by nature, they do occasionally come to the surface in shoals and can be taken on fly. Though their presence was widely known, they had no benefit of close season in Britain until the mid-19th century, and even now few anglers are interested in them.

The days are long since past when lochs were netted for their superfluity of char for salting and drying for the winter. Tales of this practice were graphically related in Hardie's *Ferox and Char*, for instance in the

little stream that runneth between the two lochs [Loch of the Lowes and St Mary's Loch] . . . yet at that season the countrey people with plaids sewed together like a net take such stock of them in vessels for the food of their families.

This was probably in the late 17th century; Stoddart did not mention them when he wrote about his visit to the same lochs in 1830.

In America too, some lakes had a superfluity of small char, but such were the depredations wrought for the sake of fertilizer and livestock feed that now they are extremely scarce.

Conservation bodies are aware that char are susceptible to environmental pressures – not necessarily from over-fishing with rod and line, since they do not have the attractions of trout to many anglers. All the same, stocking is sometimes carried out. The Scottish newspaper, the *Hawick Reporter*, featured on its front page a recent char-stocking exercise in the Borders. Arctic char from one of the last lowland strongholds,

GREAT LAKE TROUT.

Loch Doon in Dumfries and Galloway, were released early in December 1987 into Talla Reservoir. More will follow into the reservoir and into Megget in the next three years. Megget, interestingly, is a hydroelectric impoundment which feeds the Loch of the Lowes and St Mary's Loch, where Hardie once noted that superabundance.

BROOK TROUT

In 1880, when Day wrote his *Fishes of Great Britain and Northern Ireland*, he recorded that the brook trout had been an introduced fish in Britain for some twenty years. It seemed to thrive in most places, and even now some British fishery owners stock their waters with it. But in Britain I have never seen a brook trout with the same intensity of colour that I noticed in some small examples caught in beaver-dam country in northern Maine. Though the markings are similar, the fish in Britain seem matt and dull compared with the bright colouring of the American fish. Fish of about 2 lb, caught when we were trolling for landlocked salmon, were not very definitely coloured either; and as they were caught at the same time of year, this seems to confirm that different strains will show different characteristics.

This char is a shortlived species. Some races live for only four years, so for it to attain weights in double figures it must have a perfect habitat: plenty of food, security, water temperatures in the 57°–61°F (13°–16°C) band, and freedom from pollution. Central South America has proved an outstanding new habitat for this fish; in its native eastern seaboard of the United States and Canada only the Canadian waters can now be expected to provide regular trophy fish – and the farther north the bigger the fish.

LAKE TROUT

The third major char is the lake trout. My own introduction to this species occurred on a day when the weather whipped up Munsungan Lake in Maine to such a state that no boats other than ours ventured out. Towards a lee shore, in about twenty feet of water, the streamer I was trolling for landlocked salmon was seized by an invisible fish, which immediately headed back to the depths whence it came. Plenty of power, plenty of

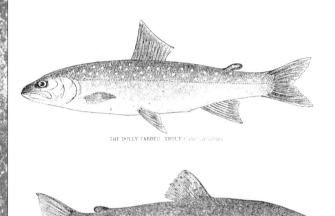

THE DOLLY VARDEN TROUT

THE BROOK TROUT (*Salvelinus fontinalis*).—A Stout Specimen—Weight ½ lb.

stamina, yet all the runs it made were vertical, not horizontal. Time and again the coloured sections of the trolling line would be reeled in, only to be pulled irresistibly into the depths. Eventually a fish emerged, brownish-olive, and scattered with pale spots, quite unlike the landlocked salmon we were hoping for. Initially we eyed it with doubt. It was only about 7 lb, yet it sparked my enthusiasm for the species: it was released, almost with affection, to think seriously about its folly in taking my fly.

Mine was not a big fish. These slow-growing, long-lived fish can attain over 100 lb, which puts them among the heaviest of the salmonids. As its lifestyle is spent in very deep water, it is essentially not a fly-fisher's fish, but the smaller ones will be found cruising in shallower water and the fly-fishing equivalent of trolled lures and spoons will take them. With their preference for cold waters, they thrive in the more northerly latitudes of North America, yet surprisingly are found nowhere in Asia.

At one time the Great Lakes were one of the prime fisheries, but when the lamprey gained access the lake trout became its prey and the population declined drastically. Lampreys are now controlled and the population is recovering. Two marginally different subspecies, the fatty siscowet and slightly less fatty humper, are also increasing their numbers again.

For that great American angling writer Al McClane, lake-trout fishing means raw days in the North Country, where only tough dwarf plants and mosses can cling to the rocks. He attributes the strongly forked tail of these fish to their need for speed, and the design of the dorsal fin, set well back, to the same purpose. He expresses a healthy respect for the lake trout's teeth – which are large and all over the mouth.

An interesting cross, which is fertile, is the splake, product of brook trout (m) x lake trout (f). It is fast-growing, matures more rapidly than the lake trout, and bears equal shares of the characteristics of both parents.

THE MUSEUM OF AMERICAN FLY FISHING

Manchester, Vermont

GILLAROO TROUT.

FROM NATURE AND ON STONE BY F. F. PALMER.   Entered according to act of Congress, in the year 1852, by N.Currier, in the Clerk's Office of the District Court of the Southern District of N.Y.   Reprinted from LITH. BY CURRIER & IVES, N.Y.

THE TROUT STREAM.

CHAPTER THREE
OTHER VARIETIES

It seemed appropriate to introduce the chars between the two major species of trout because they overlap the geographical range of each. Only by introduction do the rainbow trout species occupy the native waters of the brown, and vice versa.

RAINBOW TROUT

It would be a relief if rainbows were fish that could be defined simply, but unfortunately their classification is as complicated as their cousins'. Initially, one can at least make the distinction between the sea-run race and the landlocked.

Landlocked rainbows may, like the chars, be relics of the Ice Age. There are numerous varieties, with indubitable physical differences, but there is no real authority (for example) for scale counts along the median line as a method of subspecies differentiation. Tests have shown that low temperatures at a certain stage in the development of recently hatched young will induce higher scale counts. However, what English fishermen recognise as *Salmo shasta* – lightly spotted, with small, stubby head – really does differ from the heavier-headed, more densely spotted rainbow, and spawning times of races can differ by many months. The magenta stripe from the gill covers along the flank is a variable: more pronounced in some races and more pronounced in all as spawning time draws near.

The genetically pure rainbows in their ideal habitat are highly prized as sporting game fish. Unfortunately for the stock, rainbows domesticate all too well for fish farming, and there has been an irresponsible mixing of genes in the rush to produce competitively priced, fast-growing, hatchery fish which will produce a good return as table fish at about 10–12 oz, but whose performance is less good as a sporting fish. In general though, rainbows, with their tolerance of a wide range of water temperatures and their catholic approach to diet, are a welcome trout form. Throughout their lives they exist, in part at least, on zooplankton, a food to be expected in their smallest phases as fry and parr but rather surprising in heftier specimens.

To state that all rainbows are easier to catch than all browns would be a rash assertion, but it is accepted that they rise more freely and react less selectively. Their play is more lively (usually nearer the surface and with more leaping, which is an added

The Trout Stream, *an American north-western river, from a Nathaniel Currier print (1852).*

Fly-Fishing in America (late 1860s).

Opposite:
Catching a Trout, a Nathaniel Currier print (1854).

attraction). In Britain I prefer to see and fish for the native brown trout, but in New Zealand, for instance, particularly at Taupo in North Island, the rainbow is an exceptional game species, extremely well suited to its adopted habitat.

The migratory form of the rainbow is called the steelhead – either because of its general colouration, or perhaps because it has a strong skull. The fish darkens as it approaches spawning, and the side stripe, which may be barely perceptible when the fish is fresh-run, rapidly intensifies to the customary magenta hue.

The steelhead is generally classified as *Salmo gairdneri*, but its devotees do not pause to question its name. They are out in all weathers for what *they* consider the strongest freshwater gamefish of all, and one which can attain weights of up to 40 lb.

These fish may not need to feed in freshwater, though some choose to, but they react quite favourably to the usual range of anglers' attractions and fly patterns are legion. Mostly they are wet flies, and since depth is thought to be all-important many are tied on hooks of extra stout wire. Of bait, salmon roe is particularly attractive and many fly patterns represent single or double eggs.

In direct contrast, some people adopt the dry fly for steelhead, which clearly have the charm of unpredictability to add to their other sporting virtues.

THE CUT-THROAT

People often suppose that any silvery trout with liberal black spotting is a form of rainbow. One relation, which does have many superficial likenesses but is considered a different species, is the cut-throat. It is another inhabitant of the western seaboard of the United States and today its range widely overlaps that of the rainbow.

The 'standard' cut-throat: scientists distinguish the species from rainbows by the teeth in their throats between the gill arches; fishermen recognise the slash of red on the undersides of the lower jaw, the lack of a magenta strip on the flanks, and the more pointed lobes of the tail fin. Fifteen subspecies of cut-throat are recognised, differing in background colouring and in the size, number and brightness of their spots.

Dependent on their habitat, cut-throats reach a maximum weight of half a pound, but elsewhere may grow to 40 lb (recorded) or even 60 lb (suggested). They are fairly

CATCHING A TROUT.

Left:
Brook Trout Fishing,
Currier and Ives (1872).

unselective compared with brown trout, and susceptible to heavy fishing pressure, so well-managed fisheries insist upon catch-and-release.

Sea-run races are found, though perhaps it would be more accurate to call them 'estuary-run' since they do not travel far. As with brook trout this does not greatly boost their weight, for a landlocked cut-throat in waters rich in prey fish will soon achieve double figures. They tend, given the opportunity, to be more predacious than rainbow trout, and hybridism, which is regrettably easy, results in very rapid growth rates.

GOLDEN TROUT

Those who have climbed thousands of feet to pursue them think that golden trout are the most handsome of all the trouts. Their range is small and interest in them correspondingly limited. The literature on them is therefore sparse, though an issue of the *National Geographic Magazine* some 30 years ago contained a well-illustrated article about them.

More recently I came across a mention of them in Chuck Yeager's autobiography. He was the American test pilot who was the first to break the sound barrier, but his high-speed life left him opportunities to fish, and he too was a devotee of golden trout: 'they are so delicious that once you eat some, you'd crawl halfway to heaven to have more'.

He was involved in Operation Golden Trout, when USAF planes were 'borrowed' to fly some of these little fishes a thousand miles from the Sierras to waters in New Mexico for the benefit of Yeager's commanding officer, who was about to retire to that area.

This is another group with relict-type populations. All have a background colouring which varies in intensity from butter yellow to rich gold; the most highly coloured are normally river rather than lake fish. All are small, all have high scale counts along the lateral line (which is customary in species that inhabit high altitudes), and all provide some sport with a fly, particularly with imitations of the smaller food insects.

The South Fork Golden, *Salmo aguabonita*, is the best-known, *S. roosevelti* is not so heavily spotted and *S. chrysogaster* has less intense red markings. Taxonomists find these fish have a reasonably close relationship to cut-throats, except for *chrysogaster* which has points of similarity with rainbows. It is rare that any of the goldens achieve trophy size by the standards of other trout, but in 1948 an eleven-pounder was taken. Since their natural habitat is above 8,000 feet, fishing for them has attractions not matched in lowland waters.

THE GRAYLING

'There is a fish', said Walton, 'called by some an *Umber*, and by some a *Greyling*, a choice fish, esteemed by many to be equally good with the *Trout . . .*'

In later years grayling enjoyed a mixed reputation. In the era of dry-fly purism in England, when the trout was exalted as the only quarry fit for gentlemen, grayling was regarded as no more than vermin, to be annihilated by the most effective means available. Easier said than done, however; there are still grayling in the Hampshire chalkstreams.

In England today, the grayling is sometimes disdained because it is not a trout, in the same way as a sea-trout is (in salmon rivers) condemned for not having been born a salmon, but there are too many fishermen who regard the grayling as a true game fish for anyone to question that judgment any longer. Grayling are said to increase rapidly in numbers given favourable conditions, though there is little hard evidence that this leads to extermination of trout, but if the ratio of grayling to trout caught in a trout stream is too high, anglers tend to get restless.

Part of the trouble is that grayling spawn in late spring, and are at their least fit when trout are in prime condition. It is hardly surprising that the trout gives better 'sport' when hooked. In recent years the late Reg Richyni was a great champion of grayling. Roy Shaw has taken remarkable photographs of it during the spawning season, and Arthur Oglesby's many articles in angling magazines have made sure that its role in our sporting year is not forgotten.

The fisherman who sets out deliberately to catch grayling may well feel that the trout which takes his offering is the interloper. The trout, however, has an indigenous right

VENDACE.   GWYNIAD.   GRAYLING.

to exist in most British waters whereas the grayling is often an import, a successful colonist, which has thrived particularly on its introduction to limestone rivers and chalkstreams, in fact to any good clean water of adequate flow.

From their original eastward-flowing rivers – once parts of the post-glacial Rhine basin – grayling are now widely distributed in Britain. In these isles they do not grow large: some specimens in glass cases are over 4 lb, but a fish over 2 lb may be regarded as a trophy. In mainland Europe larger specimens are caught.

The Swiss, Charles Ritz, among them, and many Frenchmen, consider the grayling to be more exacting to fish for than the brown trout. Bill Currie has had some lively adventures with big Lapland grayling, but Lapland is rather remote for even specimen grayling.

The European grayling derives its Latin name, *Thymallus thymallus* from the belief, stated in the earliest angling literature, that it smells of thyme when fresh from the water. Males and females may be distinguished by the set of the large dorsal fin. It is larger in the male and tapers downward from back to front. In the female the fin is higher at the front. Colouration varies with locality. Usually it has a pale belly and dark back, with countershading in silvery pewter and a slight play of iridescence when the fish is out of the water.

Asia has the Kosogol grayling, and there is another subspecies known as the Mongolian grayling. Other subspecies can be found with minor differences. The New World has its grayling as well: the wide-ranging Arctic grayling, the Montana grayling, and the Michigan grayling. The latter, however, is believed to be extinct, a casualty of the logging industry – plus overfishing perhaps.

All grayling are easily identified by their large dorsal fin and strongly forked tail. They are shoaling fish, with the senior fish at the front of the shoal. They lie deep and swim up to the surface to take surface offerings (unlike trout, which hover at mid or high levels in the water), and they seem unwilling to intercept offerings to right or left of the line of drift in which they are feeding. There is no doubt about their finicky preference for tiny flies on very fine leaders, wherever they are regularly fished for.

American flies from The Printing Art (1913).

VENDACE, POWAN AND OTHER 'WHITEFISH'

Grayling used once to be classified as *Coregonus*, the genus of whitefishes, which are genuine salmonids though in general of less sporting interest than trout, char and salmon. Those who delight in the unusual or attractive appearance of the fish they choose to catch – or, perhaps more often encounter while fishing for another species, would regret my omitting to mention these interesting fish.

In the British Isles, the vendace is the most unlikely sport fish. A plankton eater, only a few ounces in weight, it is nonetheless of noble salmonid stock. It is restricted to Loch Maben in Dumfries, and neighbouring waters, having been put there, according to ancient though unlikely legend, at the instruction of Mary Queen of Scots. Like all members of the salmon family, it was originally a sea fish which became isolated during the changes that followed the Ice Age.

The houting (the name may be a corruption of whiting) is found mostly in marine waters, though it does sometimes venture into fresh water. Some taxonomists regard it as a form of the powan, gwyniad or schelly, which is quite widely distributed in northern Europe. Where feed is rich it can attain a weight of 20 lb, but the normal size is around half a pound.

Northern and broad whitefish are not found in the British Isles, but are spread throughout the north and western regions of Europe and Asia, extending to Alaska and into Northern Canada. The cisco, like the round whitefish, is better thought of as a forage fish rather than an important gamefish in its own right. The Rocky Mountain whitefish is regarded as something of a usurper and exploiter of the habitat of more desirable gamefish. All these salmonids share details such as forked tails and silvery, unspotted appearance, and resemble a herring as much as a trout.

THE MIGHTY HÜCHEN

Before we turn to the true salmon, there is one other interesting gamefish, thought to be quite low on the evolutionary scale but one which quickens the European blood. This is the hüchen, a voracious salmon, essentially a river fish which has chosen not to migrate. The hüchen (*Hucho hucho*) is also called the Danube salmon, being a native of the Danube and its tributaries.

Unfortunately, they are under considerable pressure: trophies over 30 lb are now unlikely, and the average is 4 lb to 6 lb. With hydroelectric schemes affecting upstream tributaries of the Danube, and heavy overfishing throughout the system, a hüchen of any size is a considerable prize, to be photographed and admired and immediately returned to the water!

Hüchen were introduced to the Thames in England in the 19th century, and for many years afterwards there were rumours of them being seen, if not caught. Some people believe that the truly massive trout that were occasionally taken from the Thames may, in some cases, have been hüchen. If not actually trout, however, they were perhaps more likely to have been stray salmon. There is really no excuse for error. Apart from differences in teeth, the scale count along the lateral line of a hüchen is almost twice that of a brown trout. In general, the colour is more like a salmon than a trout, silvery with a profusion of X-shaped spotting. The fish darken at the approach of the spawning season.

The taimen, which is found in eastern parts of the Soviet Union, shares the relatively primitive form of the hüchen. It can reach a huge size, over 150 lb, and it too is predacious on other fish.

CHAPTER FOUR
SALMON

The *Hucho* species are regarded as lower in the evolutionary chain than the chars, which, in turn are not as highly developed as the *Salmo* genus. The Pacific salmon are thought to be at the pinnacle.

Essentially, the trout species of *Salmo* are freshwater residents with strains which may migrate. In contrast, the salmon species of *Salmo* are normally migratory, with a few strains which stay in fresh water.

By far the most important are the migratory forms of salmon, paramount in their commercial and sporting worth, and to the eye of many anglers the most attractive of all freshwater game fish. The black and silver of an absolutely fresh-run salmon, with a bright play of iridescent lilac and turquoise, is a lovely sight.

SALMON (MALE.)

Long before Walton's day, when he called it the 'king of freshwater fish' it has enjoyed immense esteem. Though early authors generally considered it a fish of cataracts and tumultuous streams, it is also found in more peaceable settings, as the limpid watercourses of the south of England attest. Scotland and Ireland however are more suited to salmon than is England, and it is in Scotland that we find records of some of the larger fish. If William Calderwood could with confidence accept the poacher's tale of a fish of 103 lb from the mouth of the River Devon, then so can I.

SPECIMEN SALMON

A list of monster salmon appears in Frank Buckland's *The Natural History of British Fishes*, published in 1881. The Tay salmon which heads the list, elsewhere recorded as 72 lb and 71 lb, is here given as 70 lb (length 4 ft 5 in); Rhine salmon, 69 lb (4 ft 8 in); Shannon 54 lb; Tay again at 53 lb and Rhine at 51 lb and so on.

Nowadays, worldwide, a salmon over 30 lb is a trophy fish, and according to some taxidermists even 25 lb fish are quite often brought in by their captors, who regard them as trophies worth preserving for posterity. But, judging by surviving examples of stuffed fish in glass cases from around the turn of the century, 40 lb was then about the minimum weight for preservation. Whether large fish are proportionally fewer nowadays than they were when the runs of fish were bigger, I do not know. The Tweed and the Wye, where a tale is told of a monster of 80 lb or more than got away in 1920 but was later found dead, still produce very big fish occasionally. (Possibly the input of salmon parr from the Rhine in 1869 was something to do with the size that Wye fish can achieve.) The name 'portmanteau' is current there for a big fish – one of around 35 lb or more – and the rod-caught record remains Miss Doreen Davey's 59-pounder.

RHINE AND THAMES

Rhine salmon, having once been highly regarded as a prime race, are no more. Pollution of the river, which continues even now, has been their downfall. In the single season of 1879 five salmon were taken in commercial nets weighing over 45 lb.

Buckland comments: '352 lb for six salmon, viz: no less than the weight of four sheep and a half (average sized sheep) as dressed for the butcher's shop'.

In Britain, Tay and Tweed were once rivalled by Tyne, Trent and Thames. According to Izaak Walton, 'it is observed by Gesner and others, that there is no better Salmon than in England: and that though some of our Northern Countries have as fat and as large as the River Thames, yet none are of so excellent a taste.' Many later writers repeated the view that the best salmon in Britain came from the Thames.

This tradition encouraged efforts to restock the Thames with salmon in recent years – since the river has been cleaned up sufficiently. It is too early to say whether such attempts will be successful, and there are those who regard them as misguided.

Still, good catches of Thames salmon were made before the Industrial Revolution, no doubt of it. Wheeler, in *The Tidal Thames* (1979), quotes figures for annual catch of salmon at Boulter's Lock. In the ten years 1795–1804, the annual average was 32. For the decade 1812–21, however, it was only eight, and after 1824 the catch was nil. What was probably the last fish of the true Thames stock was caught in 1833. When honourable members of parliament had to meet with curtains drawn across the windows to keep out the stench from the river flowing by, the fastidious salmon had no chance of progressing through to the cleaner water upstream.

*S*almon à la Chambord,
from Le Livre de Cuisine
(c.1880).

APPRENTICES AND THE SALMON

As support for the allegation of abundant salmon in the Thames, it is often said that medieval London apprentices had a clause written into their articles which forbade their masters to feed them salmon more than once or twice a week. No one has ever actually produced such a document and, though the assertion is still frequently encountered, there seems to be no basis for it. Nevertheless, accounts of the objections of servants and other menials to a diet of salmon are too common to be dismissed. They occur in France and other countries, as well as England and Scotland. And when we think a little further, it is clear that such objections are not so odd as they seem to us, paying £4 or £5 a pound for wild salmon at the fishmonger's. For the object of the complaints was no fresh-run spring fish with the sea-lice still on it, gently poached and

*L*anding a salmon with a 'tailer' – preferable to a gaff though not to a (large) landing net.

Left:
A mature cock salmon fighting his way upstream. Illustration by Martin Knowelden from The New Compleat Angler (1983).

served cold with mayonnaise; what it was, no doubt, was the meat of lank old kelts, easily captured by more or less anyone (if not actually picked up dead), salted and stored for months in a barrel and boiled into a mushy porridge.

NORWEGIAN SALMON

Large rivers tend to produce large fish. The Irish Shannon, before hydroelectric works were built, was famous for big fish. The Tay and Tweed in Britain have produced fine trophies, and the Cascapedia in Canada has surrendered fish over 50 lb. The huge, though often short, Norwegian rivers have the finest record of all in this respect.

For sheer *joie de vivre*, Charles Ritz's tales of his angling adventures in Norway are well worth reading. More factual detail is found in the records of C.M. Wells, who caught many great fish from the Vosso, the river from which mighty salmon are still regularly taken. Odd Haraldsson's party over the past decade has caught many fish over 30 lb and a fair number over 40 lb.

Farther north, the Alta still provides phenomenal catches of heavyweight salmon, but the rod-caught record came from the Norwegian bank of the Tana or Teno, which divides the country from Finland. Here Postmaster Henrikson caught a fish of 79 lb 2 oz in 1928.

DOOMED SPECIES

The miserable story of the decline of the Atlantic salmon has been chronicled by, above all others, Anthony Netboy. Much of the damage was done long before conservation acquired its modern meaning, and before salmon fishing became a serious sport. The early writers (before the 19th century) all included salmon among the quarry of the fisherman, but few wrote with the confidence of a successful salmon fisher.

The decline of salmon rivers took place on both sides of the Atlantic. Along with shad and sturgeon, salmon were once as plentiful in the north-eastern United States as they were in Newfoundland and the rivers of the St Lawrence basin. The Algonkin

used salmon as fertiliser for their corn crops, and obligingly tipped off the Massachusetts settlers regarding this piece of husbandry. In the mid-18th century whole salmon could be bought in Boston for less than a penny a pound. But there appears to have been no sport of salmon fishing, other than spearing the fish, until about 1830, and by that time the water-devouring mills had already sprung up on the banks of many of the best rivers.

In Maine the rivers were choked by timber floating down to the sawmills, and those salmon which somehow fought through the sodden sawdust found their way blocked by dams. Despite legislation, salmon ladders were absent or ineffective. By 1886 Henry P. Wells (in *The American Salmon Fisherman*) could name only three rivers in the United States where a salmon fisherman might feel reasonably sure of success – all in the extreme north of Maine. In 1966 the U.S. secretary of the interior, issuing a list of endangered wildlife, named the Atlantic salmon as one of them.

Canada, of course, was more fortunate, despite severe over-fishing as a result of the establishment of commercial fisheries (it was said at the end of the 19th century that nine out of ten salmon caught on the fly in the Restigouche and its tributaries displayed scars from nets).

Nowadays, fortunately, conservationists have more muscle than they did then, and salmon fishermen can be a vociferous band, on occasions. It is a curious fact that the sport of salmon fishing became popular at about the same time as the salmon was disappearing from so many rivers. Some would argue a cause and effect relationship: the scarcity of salmon promoted interest in catching them.

LANDLOCKED SALMON

The standard behaviour of the Atlantic salmon is to head for the sea after two or three years in fresh water. Offshore and deep-water feeding will allow it to put on weight rapidly, and after one sea-winter (when it is commonly known as grilse) or two or more sea-winters (when it is known as salmon) the fish will return to its river of birth to spawn, with a chance of surviving to return to spawn a second time. However, there are strains which no doubt could migrate but choose not to. The ouananiche of Quebec

waters is one example. Another landlocked salmon lives in Sebago Lake in Maine, and there are landlocked races also in South America and in South Island, New Zealand.

At one time I spent many pleasant hours in shallow trolling for landlocks. They are intensely vigorous and active fighters, regularly acrobatic, and with more stamina than their size suggests. Any mention of them brings back some of the happiest fishing memories of all. Sizes were similar to British sea trout, generally 1 lb to 2 lb, with better fish over 3 lb and one or two more than 4 lb. Larger fish are of course possible; landlocks have been taken in the 20 lb range. Richness of feed is responsible, with smelt a main item in the diet, particularly just after ice-melt, but a life expectancy of over seven years is unlikely. All the mature Atlantic salmon features are there: X-shaped spotting on silver flanks, dulling at the approach of spawning time; a lower scale count than brown trout, which they much resemble; slightly concave tails, rather than convex as is found in trout.

Scandinavia also has landlocked Atlantic salmon: the Saimaa salmon is found in Finland and in Russia, the Gullspang in Sweden and the Blege in Norway. Like their American equivalents, they do not achieve the size of sea-run counterparts. There is a further long-term relict known as the Adriatic salmon, which occurs in the rivers of Dalmatia and is taxonomically placed somewhere between the Atlantic salmon and the brown trout.

PACIFIC SALMON

Many ideas have been floated regarding the relationship between the Atlantic and Pacific salmon, but none has elicited universal agreement. Many experts hold that the half-dozen Pacific species are comparatively recent off-shoots of the Atlantic salmon, who migrated to the Pacific at some time when neither land nor ice blocked the way through the Bering Strait. The gap then closed and they were isolated, eventually evolving in their new environment into a new genus.

For a long while Pacific salmon have had two main functions: for commercial canning (since 1864) and as a major food source for Eskimo and Indian peoples who catch them for salting and drying for winter subsistence. It is fair to say that only in this

*T*he fish as well as the rod seems to have been larger in Victorian times.

*S*Opposite:
almon Fishing, *Currier and Ives (1872).*

century has the sporting potential of some of these fish been fully recognised. This is particularly true when they are fresh from the sea – and all but one type are anadromous. Only in the last twenty years or so have fly fishermen taken them seriously; spinning and bait casting have always had priority.

CHINOOK

Since the sheer size of the fish is always a major attraction, the chinook should probably be considered first. A fish with a record weight of 97 lb (rod and line, 1985) and 126 lb (net) would stir any fisherman's adrenalin.

Any Pacific salmon over 20 lb is likely to be a chinook. The level at which the fish is caught in the tidal rips and estuaries may well determine its type, as the different Pacific salmon shoal and forage at different depths and chinook usually inhabit the lowest levels. Chinook are partial to large lures, particularly spoons, trolled deep. To enable tackle to be reasonably 'sporting', the line quite close to the lure is held in a quick-release device with a weight suspended on a separate line – a downrigger. When the fish strikes the lure the fishing line is freed from the restraint of the lead and its separate leader. Otherwise, the fish would have to be played with a heavy weight fixed to the line.

Spring, king, quinnat and tye are all names of the chinook (tye specifically to indicate that the fish has achieved the trophy size of 30 lb recognised by the Tye Club of Campbell River, established in 1924). Its habitat extends from the western coast of the United States to the Arctic. Its spawning runs take place regularly throughout the year.

COHO AND SOCKEYE

When the Great Lakes fisheries for lake trout were devastated by lampreys, the first move was to produce hybrid splake, which mature faster and thus have a chance to breed denied to the slow-maturing lakers by the lampreys. Then, because the alewives (the main prey fish) were becoming overpopulous, the Lakes were stocked with

Dry Fly Requisites.
Waistcoat Pocket Fly Oil Bottle.

Opposite:
Ogden Pleissner, Salmon Fishing (1950s).

Oliver Kemp Fishing in the American West *(1906). A moment all smoker anglers will recognise.*

chinook and coho. Both species adapted their anadromous habits to treat the Lakes as the sea and the inflowing rivers as their spawning grounds.

The secret of catching them in the Lakes lies in locating the level of the forage fish shoals. Where they are – and that will largely depend on water temperatures – there will be the coho and the chinook (mixed catches are possible).

The coho weighs, on average, between six and eight pounds, and it is a fair assumption that fish heavier than ten pounds are chinook. More detailed distinction can be seen in the gums: dark, even blackish, in the chinook, white in the coho. The other guide is external spotting. In the chinook the dorsal fin and both lobes of the tail fin may be spotted; in the coho spotting is restricted to the upper lobe of the tail fin.

The coho, of all the Pacific salmons, quite closely resembles *S. salar*, the Atlantic salmon, and both species have been introduced to areas outside their natural range. Cohos, however, differ from the Atlantic salmon, which do not have spotted fins. Atlantic salmon have smaller maxillaries which extend only as far as the posterior edge of the eye; and their anal fin of eight to ten rays ends in a line nearly 90° to the lateral line, whereas all Pacific salmon have a more sharply raked anal fin, of 12 to 19 rays, at a long, shallow angle.

The coho is highly regarded by fly-fishers as, although it is largely piscivorous, very fetching streamers of polar bear hair and artificial filaments can be fished to them with great success. Locally, the coho may go under the name of silver salmon, or hooknose. The rod-caught record has stood since 1947 at 31 lb.

A tin of 'red' salmon on the shelf of a grocery store will contain sockeye. The sockeye has no spots on tail or fins and only light shoulder freckling; the pink, also found canned and so indicated, has large shoulder spots matched by large spots liberally distributed on the tail. The scale count along the lateral line in this species is high – between 170 and 229. Silvery when fresh-run, both fish quickly take on the intensified tones of spawning; the pink's back humps grotesquely (with attendant kype in the males) and the sockeye acquires a greenish head and bright red body.

The sockeye offers good chance of sport: it is willing to take either fly or bait, but is best when as fresh-run as possible. Averaging 7 lb or more in weight, with a maximum of 15–16 lb, it is somewhat larger than the pink, which averages 4 lb, though the rod-caught record stands at 12 lb 9oz. The fishing gear should be scaled to suit the size and strength of the fish.

The chum or dog salmon is less attractive than either sockeye or pink. Its flesh has less colour and fat content, making it unappealing as a commercial catch, although it is both abundant and nutritious. For sport fishing it is disappointing, since it arrives in the rivers in full sexual maturity. Sizes are, on average, 5–20 lb, with a rod-caught record of 27 lb 3 oz. Flanks of both the male and female have vertical markings – red on a dull, olive-green background, which distinguish them from other Pacific salmon. It is suggested that the name 'dog salmon' arose because the species provided winter feed for Eskimo dogs.

All these Pacific salmon are anadromous; they return to their native rivers to spawn. Unlike Atlantic salmon, they never survive spawning: mortality is total, and eagles and bears then have a field day.

There is one landlocked race, the landlocked sockeye, also known as the kokanee. It never grows very large but adult fish generally weigh in at about 4 lb. It is distinguished from trout by its larger, more sharply angled anal fins, and through dentition. Light fly tackle is recommended for kokanee, though baits and other lures prove more productive. Kokanee have some value as a food fish for the larger salmonid inhabitants of a lake.

The Art of Fishing

Opposite:
W*alter Dendy Sadler A Village Celebrity (1883). Sadler was one of the most accomplished Victorian painters of fishing scenes.*

CHAPTER ONE
THE MIND OF THE FISH

Where the pools are bright and deep
Where the gray trout lies asleep
Up the river and o'er the lea
That's the way for Billy and me.

A Boy's Song, JAMES HOGG

What are the qualities in a fisherman for him to enjoy his sport to the fullest? We all want to catch fish, and we also want to take satisfaction in the way we do it. These aims are by no means mutually exclusive, but they may involved some compromise. For example, a man may prefer to fish with a fly even when he knows he stands a better chance spinning.

I cannot say that I enjoy those anthropomorphic writings which in an attempt to get under the skin of the fish are written in the first person – the sophisticated trout talking down to the naive half-pounder about the vagaries of anglers. However, when well-presented, they can make aspects of a fish's lifestyle more immediately recognisable and may suggest aspects of its behaviour that have escaped our notice. The reader may be led to consider fish behaviour in a way which had not occurred to him before.

Fishing enjoys the finest literature of any sport and, arguably at least, salmon fishing is the most distinguished branch of that literature, in fiction as well as memoirs, books on techniques etc. One of the most remarkable attempts to get inside the mind of a fish is Henry Williamson's *Salar the Salmon* (1935). It is arguably a better book than his more famous animal story, *Tarka the Otter*, written some years earlier. The hero is an Atlantic salmon, returning to its Devon river to spawn and it gives an extremely accurate portrait of river life without attributing human attributes to a fish. Williamson was a fine novelist and a fine naturalist, as well as a competent fisherman.

What he did for the Atlantic salmon was also done for the chinook by the Vancouver naturalist and author, Roderick Haig-Brown, in *Return to the River* (1942).

If we identify with a fish, or any other animal, it is impossible – would be unnatural – to avoid attributing to it qualities which are essentially human, such as bravery or cunning. I once spent an exciting afternoon on that delightful river, the Kennet, a chalkstream, watching one larger brown trout in a stretch above Marlborough. I was quite prepared to believe that this fish was a native and not a stocked fish; by its size it was impressive on any count, probably near five pounds. In a leisurely way it would intermittently cruise around its hatch hole, leaving its regular station of midwater in a counter current. Shafts of sunshine through the surrounding trees bathed the fish in an innocent spotlight. This clearly was a creature of wit and cunning: it had taken up a position in which it was aware at any time of the approach of an angler, for there was

C.F. *Tunnicliffe* Going Up to Spawn, *one of the illustrations from Henry Williamson's story,* Salar the Salmon *(1935).*

Opposite:
Robin Armstrong Sea-Trout (detail) (1989).

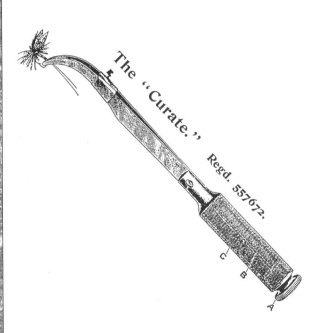

but one way to the pool among the trees and shrubs, and one place from which it could be fished. That was, I am sure, evident to the fish. The fishery rules – upstream nymph or dry fly only – precluded the most likely method of capture, a worm offered when the river was turbid with high flood water.

In fact the fish was not 'cunning', though I may have chosen that word to describe it. It was merely applying its instinct for self-preservation. Cunning demands reasoning – and a fish's brain does not have much room for developed thought. A fish relies on its senses of sight, sound and smell, to which it adds its ability to effect some sort of camouflage, and in a last resort its speed and agility in evading capture.

WHAT THE FISH SEES

Sight in a fish is at times its most important sense: the mid-brain, a proportionately large part of its brain, is devoted to this. The fish by using its eyes must identify its food and detect threats to its security. Its eye must therefore be capable of quite definite focus, for instance in registering the looming of a predator in the distance. The eye must also cope with marked differences in light values – from the darkest night of the deep waters to the blinding sunshine streaming down through shallow water on to its lidless eyes. Where the eyes are set in the fish's skull will give the angler some indications about the lifestyle of the fish. In pike the eyes are so set to give a good view upwards and forwards. It follows that a bait fished too deep will probably not be observed by the fish, while one in front of it and nearer the surface will be seen particularly well.

The typical fish's eye is in some ways like that of a human. But humans have an iris which controls how much light reaches the retina via the lens, giving either an enlarged or a pinpoint pupil at the dark centre. The fish has a fixed iris, so the dark centre is always the same size: adjustment to the light received must be made in the retina. The receptor cells in the retina are of two types: rods and cones. Cones are effective in daylight, at higher light levels, and can receive colour. The rods are more sensitive. They become effective when the light is reduced to a level at which the cones cease to work, and they operate in black and white.

Opposite:
William Garfit Hatches on the Itchen. *This is the river on which Skues evolved his theory of the nymph.*

SELECTING A FLY.

Focus is another matter. A brown trout is well equipped with muscles which can intensify short-range sight by pulling the lens closer to the retina, while at the same time the retina can still receive longer-range information. However, as the eyes are positioned to the side of the head a trout has split vision – with only a small overlap ahead and slightly upwards. Against watery backgrounds, a motionless object may not stand out very clearly. Adding a hint of movement gives a new immediacy. The trout may apply its binocular vision, which gives it perception of depth and distance, or it may turn slightly so as to focus one eye on the item for a detailed examination. Its eyes are not, however, set so far back that its own snout obscures its vision; normally, the fish swims straight at an object to intercept it.

Most of the salmonids have a pupil which appears to be round but on close examination proves to be slightly pear-shaped. Usually this pointed portion is directed by the trout towards the object in focus. In a dead fish it usually points downwards. In the grayling, this pear-shape is particularly apparent, and since the grayling is regarded as being an especially finicky taker, perhaps this precise pupil shape allows greater resolution at the front of the eye. When the grayling focuses ahead in binocular vision, it may achieve more depth of focus and better definition of detail than it would with more standard, nearly round pupils.

It's no good offering a lure which the fish cannot see, and we tend to forget that light in air differs from light in water. Take the matter of colour. However clear the water, colours lose intensity the further they are from the surface. Reds are the first to be lost, then yellow, while green is the most retentive at depth. This brings us back to the fish's watery landscape: green is the colour of its surroundings and a green object may not stand out well. White flies, baits and lures are therefore recommended for deep fishing. Black lures at the surface will stand out as silhouettes: from the viewpoint of the fish they will be outlined against any light there may be. Hence the effectiveness, so often, of black baits, lures and flies at dusk, when the fish's eye is on rod reception (perceiving light and dark only) rather than cone (which sees in colour).

THE SENSE OF SMELL

Sight may be the major sense assisting a game fish in its search for food, but its sense of smell must not be underrated; it is a very effective secondary sense. In fact, messages from its olfactory organs may alert the fish long before the prey comes into its sight. Most game fish live in clear waters where good vision is normally possible, and their organs of smell and taste remain internal, unlike bottom-feeding fish such as catfish, stirring up mud and silt, which rely hardly at all on sight for finding food.

The sense of smell is not restricted to food odours. Salmon are famous for their ability to return thousands of miles through the ocean to the river of their birth, and there can be no doubt that they locate their native river by smell. Once on their spawning beds the males are aware through smell of the females' maturity. Prey fish detect the smell of their predatory enemies, and also the scent of their own fear in the shoal, the taint of which indicates that a predator may be still in the area, after an earlier attack. Sharks typify those species which rely on smell to hunt their food; many are the tales of their following dripped or fresh blood and of their taking hooked sportfish, though recent research suggests that sharks are equipped with a variety of sophisticated sensors, attuned to movement, which we do not yet fully understand.

Tests to measure the sensitivity of smell of some fish have produced amazing results. Sockeye salmon can detect extract of shrimp in a dilution of one part in one hundred million. Pacific salmon can detect the scent of their prime enemies, seals and sea lions, at one part in eighty billion. Eels, outstandingly, can detect one particular alcohol from the presence of just one molecule in the nostrils.

Ancient superstition recommended a marksman to spit on a bullet to make it fly true and find its mark. The idea that human saliva on a fishing bait might increase its efficiency seems equally unlikely, but one scientist who taste-tested catfish found that third in attraction, after worms and liver, was human saliva!

The taste and touch sense of fish are also important to the angler. Taste and smell are akin in fish, as they are in humans. In game fish taste may in fact be largely a matter of 'feel': the spinner or artificial fly is 'wrong' in the fish's mouth. A highly taste-sensitive fish such as the catfish investigates with its external taste-feelers, or barbels, and only

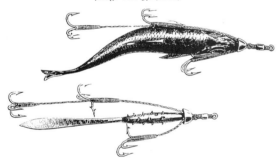

FARLOW'S IMPROVED " DEE " SPINNER.

(Reg. No. 372,600.)

Alfred de Breanski
(1852–1928).
Evening After Rain.

A de Bréanski

Opposite:
Thomas Spinks The
Bridge Pool (1876).

One of *Arthur Rackham's
illustrations for an edition of*
The Compleat Angler
(1931).

when that examination results in a satisfactory conclusion is the food item ingested. The less acceptable the feel of artificial bait or lure, the quicker the fish will reject it, and thus the quicker the angler will have to tighten!

SOUND

Water is an effective medium for carrying sound, and fish do not need external ears, which would upset their streamlining. The right sorts of sound will attract fish, while the wrong sort will induce the reflex of fright. The fish's sensitivity accords with its surroundings – whether the water is mildly turbulent, or sluggish and calm.

Apart from their internal 'ears', fish have sensitive nerve endings along their lateral lines. These provide an increased awareness of sound, which in water means water displacement, in the lower frequencies. The surface deflects most airborne noise, but the noise made by an angler striking a rock, or letting his tackle fall into the bottom of a boat, will be transmitted very effectively. For the boat-angler it is worth carpeting boat decks, soft-padding the bottom of tackle boxes, and putting a soft buffer strip along gunwales to soften any impact of oars or paddles.

A baitfish in trouble sends out attractive sounds to predatory fish, as they prefer a wounded or handicapped prey, being easier to catch than a hale and hearty one (the instinct of very living creature is to maintain itself with a minimum expenditure of effort). On this basis, a normal dry-fly artificial alighting on the water should do so without disturbance, as the natural insect would, although a grasshopper dislodged from the bank is likely to cause some commotion. Noise in one case will repel a fish and in the other attract it. A surface lure, like a baitfish out of control with all balance lost, will add to its attraction of shape by the commotion of being dragged across the water.

We know we need to keep out of sight when fishing. Fish can see us through the surface, even though the image is distorted by refraction. And we need 'to study to be quiet' as Walton urged us in 1653. We need our baits to look right and to sound right. In fly-fishing we do not need to worry much about smell, but if we remember the importance of the sense of taste-and-feel, we will avoid certain materials which are ejected immediately the fish detects that they are spurious.

Opposite:
*T*rout at Winchester *by V. Garland (d. 1903).*

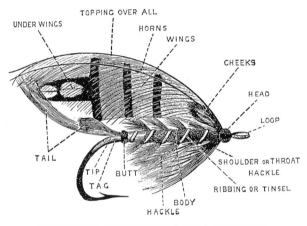

NAMES OF THE DIFFERENT PARTS OF A SALMON-FLY.

in his *Arte of Angling* (1577) had declined to discuss trout fishing for fear of offending a local 'warden' who wished to preserve his stocks. Cotton, the outstanding fly fisherman of Walton's era, thought 'a Trout affords the most pleasure to the Angler of any sort of Fish whatever', and described bottom fishing for trout as 'not so easy, so cleanly nor (as 'tis said) so Gentile a way of Fishing as with a Flie'. A century later Thomas Best insisted that 'the art of artificial fly-fishing certainly has the pre-eminence over the other various methods that are used to take fishes'.

The earliest description of artificial flies we have comes, as I mentioned in an earlier chapter, from the 15th-century *Treatyse* on angling. This list was repeated with little change until the angling 'renaissance' of the mid 17th century. Cotton's piece on fly fishing which was appended to the fifth edition of *The Compleat Angler* represents the first big advance. The most impressive fly dressings of the period, however, were given by James Chetham in *The Angler's Vade Mecum* (1681), and except for the Bowlkers in the mid 18th century, no further advances of any significance were made until the time of Ronalds in the 19th century.

The whole subject of fly-tying is an extraordinary complex one. It has been studied in obsessive detail by many learned persons. It is an esoteric art employing an unfamiliar vocabulary and demanding ingredients scarcely less strange than those alchemists' recipes recommended for making bait for bottom fish in the 17th century. As Ronalds said, 'the Dubbing Bag contains everything in the world in the way of furs, mohairs, wools, and silks'. It may include 'a little fine wool from the ram's testicles' (Alexander Mackintosh, *The Driffield Angler*, 1806) and the 'belly fur of the vixen fox stained a little pink with urine burns' (Art Flick, *The Streamside Guide*, 1947).

Building, to some extent, on the British tradition, other schools or 'cultures', of fly fishing have grown up, with the United States taking a leading place.

ATTRACTION AND DECEIT

Over the years, many hundreds and thousands of fly patterns have been devised. In broad terms, all of them can be placed in one of two categories: attractors and deceivers.

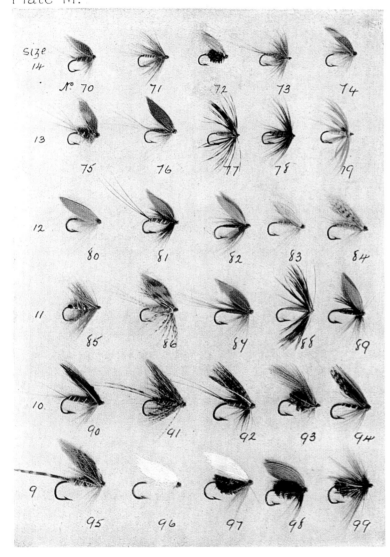

size
14

N° 70   71   72   73   74

13

75   76   77   78   79

12

80   81   82   83   84

11

85   86   87   88   89

10.

90   91   92   93   94

9

95   96   97   98   99

204   203

205   202

206   201

207

208   200

Left:
Trout and salmon flies from Farlow's catalogue (about 1910).

Members of the group considered as attractors do not necessarily bear close similarity to any natural food forms and sometimes appear to have no relationship with anything that occurs naturally in river or lake. Their design is to appeal to the predatory instinct and stimulate an attack. The deceivers, on the other hand, are intended to be close approximations to natural food forms. These two categories are merely approximate, however, and not surprisingly the boundaries are often blurred.

In the main, flies for trout and other resident fresh-water fish are deceivers. They imitate the natural food forms on which the fish depend all their lives. The migratory fish, however, are not dependent on finding food in fresh water to sustain them, and salmon flies are therefore attractors.

The saltwater diet of salmon and other migrants includes small fish and a variety of shrimps and prawns. It is not surprising, therefore, that many traditional – and for that matter modern – dressings bear at least a passing resemblance to such creatures.

My rather sweeping statement that trout fly patterns tend to be deceivers must also be qualified. Once upon a time, British trout were all brown trout, and most anglers, especially southern anglers, would agree that the brown trout is pre-eminently a fish to be deceived rather than attracted. But nowadays there are other considerations, notably the prevalence of rainbows.

Rainbow trout were first seen as a commercial food source, being relatively easy to rear in economic numbers. Their sporting properties soon became apparent, and they proved to be highly suitable fish with which to stock new fisheries. The rainbow, however, reacts favourably to attractor patterns, and brought with it from North America a whole array of attractor patterns.

THE SIZE OF THE FLY

The aim of the fish, broadly speaking, is the lowest possible output of energy combined with the highest possible input of food. For the fish, it is worth an extra effort to pursue a bigger and more nourishing mouthful, but it is unlikely to spend much of its time in high-energy search of diminutive morsels.

We should fish accordingly, with flies to suit. We must also keep in mind that small

Opposite:
G.D. Armour (1864–1949)
Trout Fishing.

An illustration from a
novel Auriol's Coronet,
published in 1893.

AURIOL'S CORONET.

By EVELYN UPTON, Author of "Christmas Eve in a Crypt," etc.

GUS AND CAR FISHING IN THE HIGHLANDS.

aquatic organisms cannot move as fast as larger ones. This will guide us as to the speed at which we fish our flies.

Migratory fish choose not to feed in fresh water, or feed irregularly. The chances are higher of taking them with attractor patterns, which trigger their predatory instincts. Incidentally, they are generally to be found in a different location from resident fish. They seek a lie which costs them the least effort in keeping their station in the current, with water sufficiently oxygenated to maintain themselves comfortably, and adequate security. A knowledge of where these lies are, their depth and temperature, is therefore a great help.

It is obviously worth having a detailed knowledge of the diet of species which are feeding, but we also need to know at what stage in its life cycle a given insect is attracting the trout. What may look like surface rises to hatched flies may in fact be fish intercepting an insect in its immature form just short of the actual surface.

WET OR DRY

Artificial flies may be divided into two other, more familiar categories – wet and dry.

The wet fly has the longer history and refers to any fly which is fished below the surface of the water. Research suggests that a trout takes between 70 and 90 per cent of its food below the surface. It is generally assumed that the dry fly had to wait until tackle, and especially lines, evolved sufficiently for the technique to be practicable, although, as we have seen, there is some argument over when this decisive step took place. A dry fly is fished either in the surface film or cocked up above the surface.

Nowadays the accomplished angler uses all dimensions of the water and fishes upstream or down as conditions or fishery rules dictate. Until the second half of the 19th century, the majority of fishermen fished downstream. A memorable advocate of upstream fishing was W.C. Stewart, whose *The Practical Angler* (1857) was by way of being a manifesto for upstream fishing ('The great error of fly-fishing as usually practised . . . is, that the angler fishes down stream, whereas he should fish up'). Stewart's message was by no means as novel as he seems to have thought, although there is no doubt that downstream casting was the common method, being on the

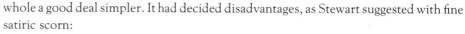

Left:
Frank Wallace The Falls Pool, Helmsdale *(Sutherland), (about 1928). The angler is the Hon. Mrs Robin Grosvenor, and the gillie is her chauffeur and butler.*

whole a good deal simpler. It had decided disadvantages, as Stewart suggested with fine satiric scorn:

> What then must be the astonishment of the trout when they see the tiny insect which they are accustomed to seize as it is carried by the current towards them, crossing the stream with the strength and agility of an otter?

The main advantage of upstream fishing, though, is that the fisherman is behind the fish, which therefore does not see him coming.

Stewart, whose river was the Tweed, used lightly dressed, soft-hackled flies which he called 'Spiders'; the agitation caused by the current created an impression of feebly struggling legs and wings. The idea that the artificial fly should imitate the *motion* (never mind the precise appearance) of the insect received powerful encouragement.

DRY FLY AND SALMON

Migratory fish were formerly offered wet flies exclusively, but in some conditions we now find that a well-presented dry fly will outcatch a wet fly. Atlantic salmon, sea-trout and steelhead can show spectacular sport on a dry fly, which often incites a more dramatic fight from the fish: having come to the surface to take the fly, they fight on the surface. This is not a hard and fast rule, but it adds to the pleasure and excitement of the sport to see the fish come up to take the fly, a sight usually denied those who fish deep and distant in dark waters.

For some fishermen, seeing the fish in its lie, casting to it, and seeing it take, is immeasurably more fulfilling than waiting for something to happen deep under water. It has to be said, though, that in waters which hold big fish an underwater take is thrilling – that sudden tug which may mean a glass-case size salmon.

SOME THOUGHTS ON FLY-TYING

In Britain since the days of Halford and Skues, I think it is true to say that, although there has been consolidation and refinement of method and detail, there has been little fundamental innovation in fly fishing. Old methods have undergone fresh scrutiny.

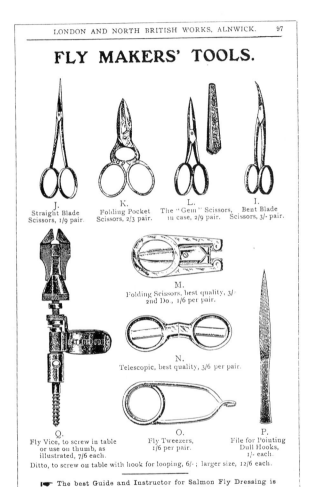

FLY MAKERS' TOOLS.

J.
Straight Blade
Scissors, 1/9 pair.

K.
Folding Pocket
Scissors, 2/3 pair.

L.
The "Gem" Scissors,
in case, 2/9 pair.

I.
Bent Blade
Scissors, 3/- pair.

M.
Folding Scissors, best quality, 3/-
2nd Do., 1/6 per pair.

N.
Telescopic, best quality, 3/6 per pair.

Q.
Fly Vice, to screw in table
or use on thumb, as
illustrated, 7/6 each.
Ditto, to screw on table with hook for looping, 6/-; larger size, 12/6 each.

O.
Fly Tweezers,
1/6 per pair.

P.
File for Pointing
Dull Hooks,
1/- each.

☞ The best Guide and Instructor for Salmon Fly Dressing is
"Salmon Fishing" by J. J. Hardy, 6/4 post paid.

Further thought has been given to such matters as detached bodies; experiments have been made with knicker elastic, nylon, and even extrusions of Dow-Corning bath-tub sealant. Research has continued, knowledge has grown, but principles have changed rather little.

Although no-hackle flies have been with us for a long time – an obvious example is the Gold-ribbed Hare's Ear – great attention has been paid to the set of wings, the pricking out of the body material and the spread of tail fibres to make the style remarkably good floaters. Italy certainly now has many fans of this style, though probably the Americans Swisher and Richards should take the credit for rekindling interest in these patterns.

The traditional tyings with traditional materials still account for the mass of the market, and it is obvious that the favourite patterns of a country often are very closely related to the most easily available materials. It is interesting to note, by the way, that countries which have the same natural insects often have very different artificial imitations of them!

Salmon wet flies have turned the full cycle of fashion. In their early days it was, again, not so much fashion which dictated their style as the availability of materials. Furs, hairs and feathers came from domestic animals, beasts of the chase and farm stock. The results were flies which were like the trout flies of the day, but larger, simply because salmon are larger fish! The Victorians convinced themselves (and apparently convinced the fish too) that what the fish really wanted was the most intricate combinations of fur and feather, with sparkling tinsels and rainbow hues. More prosaic fishermen of a later period begrudged the cost of these fancy confections and embarked on a return to more sombre types, with apparently no less, if no greater, success than their predecessors.

But what makes a really good fly, whether it represents a common aquatic insect which is readily taken by trout, or is an attractor pattern to tempt a creature which does not feed in fresh water?

There are several desiderata, any one or combination of which may at some stage be decisive in attracting at least the fly-tier, if not his quarry.

Among the requirements for a wet fly, some or all of the following features may be

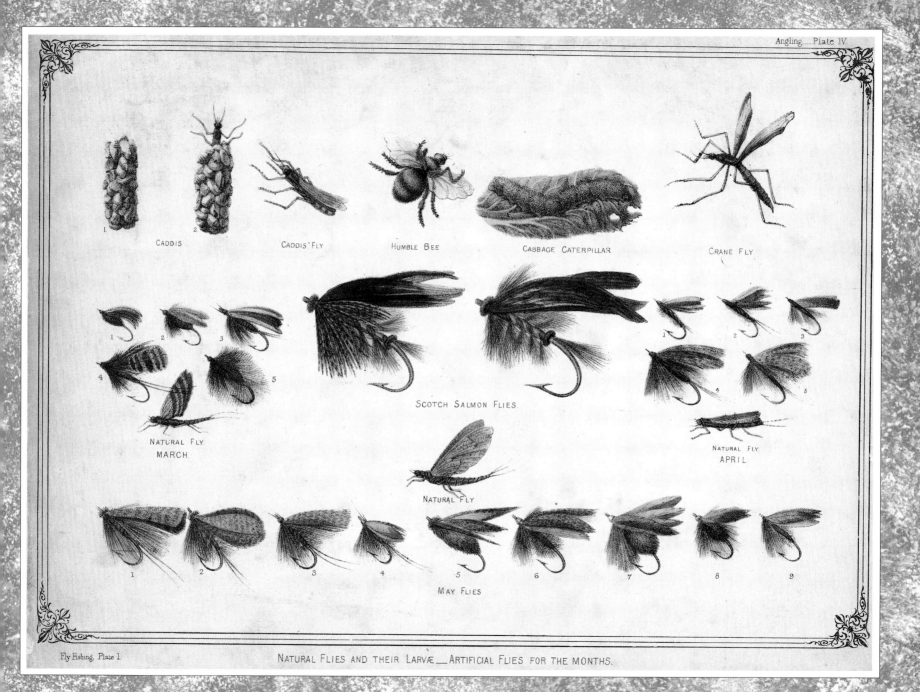

CADDIS

CADDIS FLY

HUMBLE BEE

CABBAGE CATERPILLAR

CRANE FLY

SCOTCH SALMON FLIES.

NATURAL FLY
MARCH.

NATURAL FLY
APRIL

NATURAL FLY

MAY FLIES

NATURAL FLIES AND THEIR LARVÆ ___ ARTIFICIAL FLIES FOR THE MONTHS.

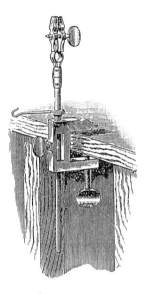

Left:
'The Dubbing Bag', says Ronalds, 'contains everything in the world in the way of furs, mohairs, wools and silks'.

A fly-tier's vice.

decisive: colour, shape, translucency, mobility, size, fluorescence, posture (whether it can be presented at the right angle – a midge pupa hangs vertically and a minnow swims horizontally) and the right movement (whether angler-induced or a function of chosen materials).

Likewise for a dry fly, size, colour, shape or silhouette, high float (if necessary), right movement, the right plane, the right angle at which the fly sits on the surface, and the right 'footprint' (the way in which the fly disturbs the surface pattern of light), visibility (either to the fish or to the angler) and iridescence (the play of sunlight on fibres giving a spectrum effect) are additional possible requirements (the last of these, like fluorescence, is not much researched and remains largely an area of surmise).

The variety of flies in unlikely to diminish. We know or think we know what we are seeing when we look at a fly; we can only surmise what the trout or salmon sees, and at no time can we ever prove why a particular fish took a particular fly.

That is the best thing about the sport – we shall never know. But we shall go on supposing, suggesting, arguing, discussing – and fishing.

THE PERIPATETIC FLY-TIER

An ability to tie one's own flies is not only helpful but is also a wonderful adjunct to the sport. Usually the tools and materials are kept at home, but a small travelling kit is worth having in the car, if not at the bankside. A vice can usually be attached to the bottom of the steering wheel without causing damage. The passenger seat can then display the range of materials needed, and a few flies to meet the exigencies of the moment can be concocted.

The challenge in fishing for resident trout lies in identifying the foodstuff and in imitating it well enough for the species to find it attractive. For reasons known only to them the fish can be so discriminating that what answers well on one day may prove futile on another, when to our senses all the conditions seem identical.

For the migratory fish, however, there come moments in their sojourn in freshwater when they will react to almost any offering, any fly of any size or colouring. At the other extreme there seem to be times when nothing excites them. In between is the range of fish which may well react if the angler has the requisite knowledge, technique and intuition born of experience.

It is a sad fact that in Scotland now the catch at the end of a six-day salmon fishing holiday averages but two fish. The really experienced fishermen tend to improve on this, but very often novices fall sadly short. Most of the salmon taken are not the 'easy' ones, but come from the intermediate class which make considerable demands on the fisherman's skill.

CASTING THE FLY

The advent of good power-to-weight materials such as glass fibre and carbon fibre has extended the range of casting, in which the work must be done by rod and line, not by weights (including the weight of the lure). There are limits to the size of an artificial fly which, though it can be tied exceedingly small – say, about as small as a couple of letters of print in this book – cannot be tied much above three inches. The limits are imposed by leaders, which tend to be overbalanced by the largest fly sizes.

Because modern carbon rods have extended the casting range, in the past couple of decades an esoteric interest in fly fishing for big game fish has developed. It is possible that more orthodox, traditional methods would produce easier catches, but this is an example of the method being more important to the fisherman than its results.

Two factors have greatly increased the popularity of fly fishing in recent years – the discovery of how to transport fish ova and, springing from that, the import of brown trout to North America and rainbow trout to Britain. Once it was seen how large the market was all suitable waters received stocks. In Britain, fly fishing for trout has ceased to be a hobby of the reasonably well-to-do. The man (occasionally woman) whose father was restricted to coarse fishing may now go fly fishing for trout in reservoirs at moderate cost.

'A *Good Day' August 1936.*

Opposite:
A *request for assistance, from a drawing by* A. Hopkins *printed in* The Graphic *(1885).*

The old man and the sea – Ernest Hemingway with a marlin.

BIG GAME

As Lee Wulff has put it, 'a fish is too valuable to catch only once'. That goes for most game fish, including the saltwater species. Sailfish can be caught and tagged and caught again many times, and there seems to be evidence that they are not unduly harmed by this. (Atlantic salmon approaching spawning *must* be returned to the water, even though the season may extend into late autumn and it may still be legal to take them.)

There is perhaps an inconsistency in wanting to hunt something to catch it and then return it to the water. But it is equally inconsistent to pursue a diminishing species and then eat the catch. However you feel about your fishing, you will agree that your interest ought to be beneficial.

In Britain most sporting fish taken on a fly are salmon and trout. Lefty Kreh's *Fly Fishing in Salt Water* has revealed how many saltwater fish will take a fly, though he discusses warmer waters than the English Channel or the North Sea. The sea quite as much as fresh water has long been a place to enjoy fishing, but fly-fishing for saltwater species was a minority sport until very recent times. There has been rapid acceleration of this branch of angling in the past couple of decades.

Saltwater fish boast many sporting qualities. The bonefish is fast and possesses notable stamina; the powerful permit also has remarkable staying power, though its unwillingness to take a fly is legendary and infuriating. These and other coastal species make outstanding fly-rodding quarry.

Among the deeper water species, tarpon is considered to be the finest fish of all on fly tackle. Tarpon are active and acrobatic when hooked, and they can achieve immense size. As it is not a favoured fish for the table, it is treated as a catch-and-release species. Good guides encourage this and are experienced at doing it in a way that leaves the fish with minimum damage and a maximum chance of recovery.

The all-tackle world record weight for tarpon is 283 lb, but on a fly rod with 16 lb breaking-strain leader a fish of 188 lb was taken in 1982, and on as light tackle as 12 lb B.S. a fish of 167 lb has been taken. The rod, needless to say, is somewhat huskier than a regular trout rod, and the reel must have a huge line capacity, a very smooth braking system and resistance to salt water.

U p Stream, *from a*
postcard of about 1920.

With these, or indeed lesser fish, it is sad to go abroad relying on hire outlets or tackle stores in the major fishing centres. The really keen fisherman may well have a 'smuggler' type of fly rod which can be dismantled into many short sections so as to fit inside a suitcase. With a couple of reels with spare spools and a choice of lines, suitable leader materials, and flies either brought from home or bought locally, fishing may be possible at short notice – and for a species not encountered at home. Very often a holiday can offer a little fortuitous fishing if you have your tackle ready, although the better way is to organise the holiday around the fishing rather than the other way about.

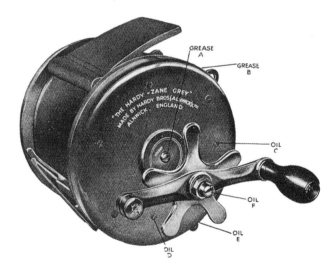

H ardy's 'Zane Grey' reel,
designed for the famous
author/angler.

LUNCHEON

A SATISFACTORY EVENING

HALF-A-DOZEN CASTS AT DAYBREAK

A DISAPPOINTMENT

A NORWEGIAN KITCHEN

A MOMENT OF UNCERTAINTY

KOLDT VAND IMORGEN

FISHING UNDER DIFFICULTIES

A RUN FOR LIFE, ENDING IN A KILL IN THE OPEN

THE SORT OF THING YOU READ ABOUT, BUT VERY SELDOM SEE

A PRETTY VISITOR HOOKS HER FIRST FISH

TAILING A TEN-POUNDER

SALMON-FISHING IN NORWAY

Fishing Around the World

INTRODUCTION

For Angling may be said to be so like the Maathematicks, that it can never be fully learnt.

ISAAK WALTON, *Epistle to the Reader*

*T*rout fishing in the Highlands, a romantic view from Lancelot Speed's Sporting Pictures (1912).

Al McClane's *The New Standard Fishing Encyclopedia and International Fishing Guide* is the best general guide to fishing around the world. The following is merely a brief summary of possibilities. Few national tourist departments are unaware of the revenue which visiting anglers can bring, and most are well equipped to deal with general fishing enquiries. They can also supply details of the leading angling journals of their country, and from such sources, as well as press advertisements, it is possible to pick the area to visit and find out which camps, guides and outfitters should be contacted.

Few national tourist departments are unaware of the revenue which visiting anglers can bring, and most are well equipped to deal with general fishing enquiries. They can also supply details of the leading angling journals of their country, and from such sources, as well as press advertisements, it is possible to pick the area to visit and find out which camps, guides and outfitters should be contacted.

GREAT BRITAIN AND IRELAND

ENGLAND is chiefly noted for its trout fishing, especially the chalk streams which gave birth to the dry-fly and nymph conventions that have spread worldwide. Most of the natural trout waters were originally inhabited by brown trout: introductions of grayling followed, and then rainbow trout. With the increase in reservoirs like Blagdon and Chew a modern tradition of stillwater fishing has grown up with sunk line and lures for brown trout and especially rainbow trout. The Midlands have the largest fisheries, like Grafham and Rutland Water which host the rapidly developing competitive side of fly fishing for trout.

On the south coast the lower reaches of the Avon and Test offer creditable salmon fishing, and the major rivers of Devon and Cornwall can offer good fishing for salmon and sea trout. The north has suffered badly from disease and commercial netting offshore still gives rise to concern. The English netting stations take a massive toll of fish migrating to Scottish waters, and the style of netting employed is forbidden in Scotland, where there is understandably fierce criticism of the practice.

SCOTLAND The four main salmon areas are the Aberdeenshire Dee, the Spey, the Tay and the Tweed, but there are plenty of other rivers which have their enthusiasts – Findhorn, Beauly, Deveron, Dionard and many others. Each has its own individual character.

For the best trouting nowadays one must turn to the lochs. Ferox, despite what the scientists claim, is still patrolling the depths of the deepest and largest lochs like Loch Awe and Loch Rannoch. Lakebound char are still to be found by those interested in them, and sea trout offer special thrills.

WALES There can be no race more skilled than the Welsh in their ability to take salmon by all fair methods, while Welsh sea-trout fishing can be exceptional. The Dovey has a name for great sea trout; the Conwy, Dee, Towy and Teifi are well known, and we cannot overlook the Usk or the Wye, a big river with big fish.

IRELAND The Blackwater in Cork is the most notable spring river, though (an old refrain) its quality is less than in past years. The Shannon has been ruined by the hydroelectric scheme. Great trout still rise in the summer in the mayfly loughs like Conn, Ennel and Mask. In the north the River Bush is showing good returns and the Foyle system is still productive. Some stillwaters are particularly good for salmon, and lough techniques like dapping can be a refreshing change from river fishing. Last but not least, Ireland is not too expensive.

EUROPE

AUSTRIA's lakes and rivers contain a variety of salmonids which take a fly readily. The Traun has excellent grayling as well as trout. Other rivers of note are the Salza, the Mur, the Lammer, the Enns and the Alm.

BULGARIA is not much noted as a fly-fishing country, though my experiences there lead me to believe there is considerable potential. I took a fly/spinning combination rod and some reels and spools with me when I was invited by the Tourist Office to assess the potential of Bulgarian hunting for the British market, and never in my life have I seen trout so willing to take a fly. In fact they showed far more interest in my Cinnamon and Gold than in a Mepps spoon, and rarely does one see trout when hooked 'tailwalk' like sailfish or marlin. Our catch earned us liberal quantities of Bulgarian champagne back in our hotel.

FRANCE In France salmon are now rare and precious. Once there were salmon in abundance in all the major rivers, but weirs, pollution, and hydroelectric schemes without adequate fish passes have taken a fatal toll.

Trout fishing is widespread both in rivers and lakes, Grayling are highly favoured, and char are found in some localities.

GERMANY once had the mightiest salmon river in Europe, the Rhine, but they have long since been exterminated. Modern German trout fishers, fly-tiers and tackle dealers are extremely skilled and inventive, and the best trout and grayling fishing is in Bavaria and the Black Forest. Browns, rainbows and grayling are widely distributed. Some of the Rhine tributaries and lakes offer trout fishing, as do the Harz mountains.

SPAIN is the furthest south of any country with a regular run of salmon. There are a dozen or so rivers along the northern coast which still offer reasonable fishing for both locals and foreign anglers.

On my visit to the rivers Cares and Deva near Santander, the brown trout were small and game, and the salmon, fresh-run after a small spate, were sleek and lustrous, in harmony with the almost turquoise waters of the Cares from which they were taken.

YUGOSLAVIA is renowned for fast-flowing streams, which produce excellent fish. The scenery, the size of the fish, the variety of species (brown trout, rainbow trout, marbled trout, grayling and maybe hüchen) are equally attractive.

Salmon mayonnaise.

AUSTRALASIA

AUSTRALIA has few rivers but where there are waters which have acceptable temperatures, flow and food for trout, both browns and rainbows thrive. Lake Eucumbene, a huge catchment reservoir in the Snowy Mountains of New South Wales, has become one of the most noted waters, attractive to all-tackle fishermen. The flyfishers bring nymphs, ants, lures, imitations of dragon-flies, hoppers and beetles, Muddlers, New Zealand-style Matukas and any other flies they think might take fish. Lake Jindabyne is another first-rate water, though considerably smaller; it has landlocked salmon and brook trout. Among the native fish which are willing takers of a fly, barramundi, with a rumoured top weight of 595 lb, might just be included, though bait and spinner are usual methods.

TASMANIA has reservoirs with good food supplies which have produced magnificent brown trout to all types of fishing, but fly hatches, of mayflies and sedges, are quite dependable. Great Lake and Penstock Lagoon are also favoured by fly fishermen.

NEW ZEALAND is one of the best of all countries for brown and rainbow trout. Rainbows are found mainly in the North Island and browns in the South Island. Lake Taupo and the Tongariro River are engraved on the hearts of many fishermen who have fished the North Island, though there are many equally good, and not so tourist/angler-frequented, lakes and rivers. Rivers south of Canterbury have the Pacific chinook salmon, which is called quinnat in the southern hemisphere. It is well established as a sporting fish, though it is primarily a spinning quarry. The introduction of the Atlantic salmon has not proved so successful. The landlocked form is found flourishing in Lake Te Anau. Guides are essential if the visiting angler wishes to venture off the beaten track; they will arrange for float planes and even helicopters. Night-time fishing is often extremely productive, particularly where the rivers flow into the lakes, and shooting-head techniques are worth learning in advance of a New Zealand trip. New Zealand's specialised techniques of fishing a sunken lure and some of its fly-tying styles are finding their way into the British repertoire.

SCANDINAVIA

FINLAND Sad to relate there are now few salmon rivers of repute. The largest, the Teno (the Tana in Norway) is the national boundary in the north. Harling is the usual technique on this massive river.

ICELAND The fish are fresh-run from the sea and the waters are free of pollution, so the salmon and the anadromous char fight harder than can be believed. Average sizes, however, are not much over 10 lb, with a few fish reaching 30 lb. There are good trout and char in the lakes with, apparently, some relict species such as the *murta* and the *depla* which seem to be a sort of proto-char. There has been to date no outbreak of salmon disease in Iceland and the authorities are determined it shall not occur. All visiting anglers must therefore disinfect their tackle and carry an official certificate stating that it has been done.

Just about every salmon river of note in Iceland is called the Laxa. *Lax* means salmon and the suffix *a* denotes river. Late July, which is the best time of year, is always heavily booked. Though the season opens in June, a trip that early is not recommended.

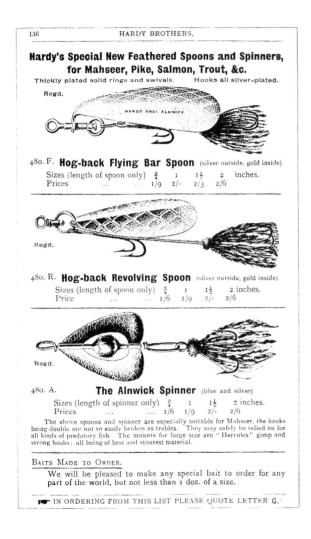

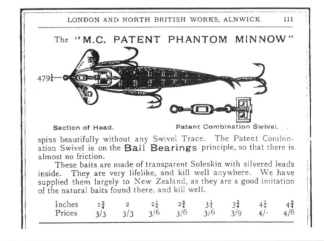

A *Norwegian river in 1870.*

NORWAY has massive rivers, massive salmon and massive rents. Here is the finest salmon fishing in the world for size of fish, but the best rivers, like the Laerdal, Namsen, Aaro, Alta and Vosso, are world-famous. Some of the lesser rivers produce excellent sea-trout as well as salmon fishing, though the average size is nothing like the Vosso's or the Alta's. Water levels depend on snow melt, and only satisfactory river heights permit the fish to run.

SWEDEN Southern Sweden has suffered from industry but in the north there is still outstanding grayling and trout fishing. The salmon fishing has declined but there is still some fine sea-trout fishing to be had. Acid rain has fatally affected many lakes and rivers. The Swedes have accomplished marvels with their massive salmon-smelt rearing programmes, which bolster the Baltic fishery.

AFRICA

The Nile perch is hardly a game fish, but since it can achieve a weight of over 200 lb, it has a certain attraction. The widely distributed tigerfish is a more likely quarry for the fly fisherman and offers good sport. Fish up to 125 lb have been reported, but the all-tackle record is 71 lb 10 oz from the Zaire River in 1985.

Introductions of brown and rainbow trout have only succeeded in the mountainous headwaters of African rivers. They can be found in Ethiopa, Malawi, Kenya and Tanzania and most notably South Africa, which has also introduced bass.

The principal trout streams are those within about 100 miles of Cape Town; some streams in the Humansdorp – Port Elizabeth areas; the Alice, Cathcart, Keiskamma-hoek, King William's Town and Stutterheim districts; upper tributaries of the Orange River system in the Barkly East area; and the Drakensberg streams flowing to the Indian Ocean.

SPORTING SERIES
"Where the speckled Trout abound."

SPORTING SERIES
SALMON FISHING. "LANDED"

Postcards purveying the charms of fishing in North America.

NORTH AMERICA

UNITED STATES Most of the salmonids flourish within the United States, besides other freshwater fish which take a fly quite readily. Alaska has large commercial canneries of Pacific salmon. Sport fishermen have to rely for the most part on bush pilots to take them to their camps and fishing grounds. Species include chinook, coho, sockeye, dog and pink salmon, rainbow and cut-throat trout, Dolly Varden and Arctic char. Among the whitefish is the inconnu or sheefish, the only predatory whitefish. Brown trout are now almost ubiquitous, being regularly found in brook-trout country and in rainbow and cut-throat waters. The rainbow in turn has spread from its western-seaboard origins throughout North America.

Florida is rapidly becoming a great attraction to foreign anglers. Good bass fishing is one draw; the other is the excellence of the sea fishing.

Rather as Britain has the fabled Test and Itchen, and Spey and Dee, so there are 'ambition' rivers in North America, with a special appeal for Americans themselves and for their visitors. New York's most famous trout stream is the Beaverkill. Brook trout gave way to browns in the Beaverkill at the turn of the century, but this river and others in the locality have generous hatches of mayfly to which the fish respond well. The LeTort gained its fame both from its good trout and the diversity of insects which form part of their diet.

On the western seaboard, the Madison is Montana's best known trout river. Stonefly hatches are a feature of most western river fishing. The Snake River in Idaho produces tantalising rainbows, and rivers such as the Skykomish, the Umqua and the Upper Klamath are prime waters for steelheads.

CANADA provides a wealth of fresh-water game fish: brown trout, brook trout, rainbow trout and char in landlocked and migratory forms; Atlantic and Pacific salmon and various whitefish. Float planes are needed to reach many waters, and small, fast, outboard-powered boats, though there is much pleasure to be had from using traditional Canadian canoes where available. For our landlocked salmon fishing we used a square-stern canoe with an outboard motor.

*T*rout fishing in the Adirondacks.

A spectacular day's catch.

Left:
*Salmon fishing in Maine,
from* Harper's Monthly
(1886).

Lee Wulff emphasised in his *The Atlantic Salmon* that on the eastern seaboard these fish are extremely acrobatic. Alan Mann, a keen salmon fisherman from Britain, found that on the Miramichi it is necessary to bring the fly over the fish very slowly in high summer, taking the mended greased-line technique to the ultimate. Another attraction of these rivers is that the salmon will take a dry fly so well. Atlantic salmon are fished for under very strict regulations controlling limits and enforcing the return of fish to the water. This catch-and-release principle is widely practised throughout the country.

SOUTH AMERICA

ARGENTINA has proved to be an ideal country for colonisation by trout. Brown, rainbow and brook trout now grow to impressive weights. The landlocked salmon has taken hold of the River Traful. Rivers tend to be turbulent, therefore well-presented wet-flies and streamers offer a better chance than dry flies, particularly as insect hatches are less of an attraction than other subaquatic food forms.

San Carlos de Bariloche is the main angling centre, with guides and transportation available. Based on Junin de los Andes, the international fly fisherman will find excellent sport in the Malleo, Quilquihue, Collon-Cura, Chimehuin and Alumine. Further south, access becomes more difficult.

BRAZIL offers an impressive length of coastline and some equally impressive large rivers. The estuaries contain tarpon, while further from the land are sailfish, blue and white marlin, yellowfin tuna, swordfish and others. Freshwater species include the dorado, which looks like a very stocky, golden, Atlantic salmon, though it is much more predatory and not fully migratory. Spinning is more common than flyfishing. The aruana is a schooling fish which can be taken on rod and line. Payara, closely related to Africa's tigerfish, are accounted among the most game of South American sport fishes, with weights reported to 30 lb. A species of pavon, like a brightly coloured perch, is highly regarded for its willingness to strike a lure or fly. There are said to be about 5,000 species of fish in the Amazon system, nearly half scientifically unclassified.

123

CHILE Trout introduced to this country have found the conditions entirely to their liking, and 'double-figure' fish are not uncommon. The broad, fast rivers are mostly fished from a boat. In the extreme south the fishing is marked by permanent and powerful winds, so it is wise to take tackle suited to the conditions.

Chile is also notable for its deep-sea fishing, with most of the usual gamefish. Black marlin and swordfish to very large weights have been taken.

OTHER REGIONS

The Soviet Union has not yet begun to encourage fishermen to visit the country, though there are Atlantic salmon and taimen to great weights in the west, and Pacific salmon in the east, among them the masu, which has considerable importance commercially. A number of rarer salmon, trout and grayling are found throughout this vast land.

Turkey: According to reports, there is fine trout fishing, currently little exploited.

The Bahamas are ideal for the pursuit of bonefish and permit. The deep water game fish are mostly seasonal, but nearly half of the recognised saltwater game fish are found here.

The great game fish of India is the mahseer, which has scales so large that they constitute trophies in themselves. In the north the fish are smaller and more slender; in the south they may exceed 100 lb. Larger specimens are more likely to take baits and lures than a fly.

Trout introduced to Kashmir have proved very satisfactory. Initially they were brown trout, but rainbow are also suited.

*T*arpon fishing in Florida.

GAME-FISHES OF THE FLORIDA REEF.

TARPON-ANGLING.

A 57lb mahseer from the Ganges, about 1900.

Acknowledgements

The publishers would like to thank the following organisations and individuals for their kind permission to reproduce the photographs in this book:

The American Museum of Fly-Fishing: 25; 45; 53; 55; 59; 60; 62; 77; 79
Barnaby's Picture Library: 76
Thomas Bewick: Preface; 29; 103
Bridgeman Art Library: 8; 15; 18; 34; 95; 97
John Buckland: 17; 32
Christie's Fine Art Auctioneers: 28
Fine Art: 51; 82; 91
Mary Evans Picture Library: 10; 11; 22; 63; 66; 71; 75; 80; 114b; 116; 121; 122; 124; 127
Farlow Ltd: 14; 19b; 33; 46; 48; 72; 90; 98; 107; 114a; 125
Hamlyn: "Going Fishing" by Negley Farson (illustrated by C.F. Tunnecliffe): 40
House of Hardy: 20; 24; 30; 36; 50; 64; 78; 86; 88; 99; 104; 116; 118a; 118b
Hulton Deutsch Collection: 21; 35; 42; 94; 105; 106; 110; 112; 119
The London Library:
   "The Complete Angler" by Izaak Walton: 16
   "British Freshwater Fish" by Rev. W. Houghton (illustrated by A.F. Lydon/engravings by
     Benjamin Fawcett): 41; 43; 49; 54; 57; 65; 67; 69; 70; 81
The Malcolm Innes Gallery: 2, 93
Mansell Collection: 6; 100
Derek Mills: 74; 111a; 117; 120; 123; (117 & 123 reproduced courtesy of Willow Books
   from "The Fishing Here is Great")
National Railway Museum: 31; 115
Peter Newark's Western Americana: 19a; 58; 61; 109
Orbis: "The New Compleat Angler" by Stephen Downes (illustrated by Martin Knowelden)
   – reprinted by Mcdonald & Co.: 72
The Salmon & Trout Association:
   "The Compleat Angler" by Izaak Walton (illustrated by James Thorpe): 12; 13
   "The Fly-Fisher's Entomology by Alfred Ronalds: 26
   "A Quaint Treatise on Flies & Fly-Making": 23
   "The Compleat Angler" by Izaak Walton (with illustrations by Arthur Rackham): 92
Sotheby's Auctioneers: 44; 52
The Spink Gallery: 37; 101; 102
The Oliver Swann Gallery: 47; 87 (paintings by Robin Armstrong)
Topham Picture Library: 108
The Tryon & Moorland Gallery: 38; 85; 89
Wellfleet Press: "Favourite Flies and their Histories" by Mary Orvis Marbury: 9; 27; 39; 83;
   113